GOD culture

GOD
culture

— BOOK ONE —
Understanding the Almighty SERIES

John A. Naphor

NEW YORK

GOD culture

BOOK ONE of *Understanding the Almighty* SERIES

© 2014 John A. Naphor.

Published in New York, New York, by Morgan James Publishing. Morgan James and The Entrepreneurial Publisher are trademarks of Morgan James, LLC. www.MorganJamesPublishing.com

The Morgan James Speakers Group can bring authors to your live event. For more information or to book an event visit The Morgan James Speakers Group at www.TheMorganJamesSpeakersGroup.com.

FREE eBook edition for your
existing eReader with purchase

PRINT NAME ABOVE

For more information,
instructions, restrictions, and
to register your copy, go to
www.bitlit.ca/readers/register
or use your QR Reader to scan
the barcode:

ISBN 978-1-61448-987-0 paperback
ISBN 978-1-61448-988-7 eBook
ISBN 978-1-61448-990-0 hardcover
Library of Congress Control Number:
2013951388

Cover Design by:
Rachel Lopez
www.r2cdesign.com

Interior Design by:
Bonnie Bushman
bonnie@caboodlegraphics.com

In an effort to support local communities, raise awareness and funds, Morgan James Publishing donates a percentage of all book sales for the life of each book to Habitat for Humanity Peninsula and Greater Williamsburg.

Get involved today, visit
www.MorganJamesBuilds.com

Habitat
for Humanity®
Peninsula and
Greater Williamsburg
Building Partner

This book is dedicated to Yahweh, my Father in heaven through my Lord and Savior Jesus Christ, to my wife and my three beautiful children, and to all those who have supported, influenced and prayed for me through the years. Although you are too numerous to name you know who you are.

Table of Contents

Introduction

I cannot even begin to tell you how many times I have heard the phrase, "God works in mysterious ways," from my friends, family members, business colleagues, and even members of my own church. In fact, I used to feel that way myself. I have noticed that people seem to fall, for the most part, into one of two camps. Folks are either angry at God or, quite simply, they are apathetic toward Him, as if He does not exist at all. It seems that the more modern our society becomes, the less of a role God plays in our culture. God is being replaced with pop.

Throughout the years, there has always been "something" inside that led me to believe that I did not quite have all the information. I had heard that God was good but I had never experienced this myself. He was never a part of my culture. Was it me or was there something unseen that I just did not have any understanding of? After all, I can remember being a small child and hearing the voice of God speak to me. But where did He go? Was it my imagination? Had He left me? Had He left all of us to fall into the chaos and suffering of such a turbulent world? Something deep inside told me no.

In all of my trials and tribulations I have never been one to play the blame game. Therefore, I never attributed to God all the crazy and messed up incidents I have experienced throughout my life. I knew *I* was the problem all along and I thank God for that. At the same time, I just could not understand why so many have suffered through so many hardships and why life seemed to be so incredibly unfair if God is truly good and merciful. Sound familiar?

So let me tell you what led me to write this book. I will begin with a brief history of my early life. Like many of you, and I do realize not all of you, I had a great childhood and wonderful parents. I was a happy-go-lucky kid, but at one point I noticed something was not quite right. When I was a young boy, my fifteen-year old cousin died in a car accident. It is my understanding that she was thrown through the back windshield, resulting in the fact that they could not even open the casket at her funeral. I cannot even begin to tell you how devastating this was to my family.

Not long after this incident, my two closest uncles died. The first was hit by the drunken driver of a garbage truck while crossing Route 1 in North Brunswick, New Jersey. He had two small children. I remember my brother and me plotting the murder of the assassin while lying in bed that night. We did not go through with it.

The second, who happened to be my late cousin's father, died of a sudden and massive heart attack. He did not have any life insurance and a tremendous financial hardship was beset upon his surviving family. My beloved aunt never recovered and knowingly allowed breast cancer to ravage her until she finally befell the same fate as her long lost loved ones. "And God, you're okay with this?" was my only thought.

Then there were my own shattered dreams. In the midst of a stellar high school basketball career, of which I sank my entire life into, I slipped on a patch of ice, slamming my shin into the bottom of a car door while having a snowball fight with my friends in a McDonald's parking lot. There were six games left in my senior season. The resulting bone bruise caused me to miss the coveted one thousand career point milestone by a mere twenty-seven points while I was averaging twenty-two per game.

Even worse was my team's ousting from the county tournament due to the absence of the team's star player, me.

Just as my injury healed enough to get back on the hardwood, our dreams were dashed in the first round of the state tournament on a half court buzzer beater by a team we had crushed twice in the regular season. Also ousted were my college Division One dreams, as the last game the scouts saw was my six-minute, three-point debacle where I could not run, jump or cut. In fact, I could barely even walk. Athletics are ruthless and there is always someone else ready to fill your spot. Needless to say, my N.B.A. dreams were flushed away along with a lifetime of shoveling off snow-covered courts and playing until the lights went out.

That began my long dark spiral into drugs and alcohol. At the time, I never realized it was merely a mask for the anger and pain I was feeling due to the hopelessness of watching all of my aspirations disappear into blackness and leaving no real hope left of repairing the shattered pieces of my life. So why not just party into oblivion? That is exactly what I did. Just like basketball, I was good at it and dedicated to it.

Now don't get me wrong, these were choices I made and I cannot even stand here today and tell you that I did not enjoy it. I most certainly did. This may sound strange, but in hindsight I would not change a single thing about my past. You will understand why as you read through this book.

The point is, although it started out fun, it was hopeless and empty. For the last three years of my partying "career," I wanted to stop but I could not. Not until something changed in my life. Unbeknownst to me at the time I had to leave the party culture behind and embark upon something brand new.

That "opportunity" came in the form of being kicked out of college for "behavioral issues" and another year of partying until I finally entered Fairleigh Dickinson University. Of course, I had absolutely no idea that this was my entrance way into God Culture so I continued to party some more until I met this cute little Asian girl who later became my wife. In hindsight, I often find God's ways to be a bit comical. *"Behavioral issues"* was how God grabbed hold of me and rescued me from eternal fire. When you sit back and think about it, it is sort of bizarre.

Late one evening after a long night of partying and about two weeks before I met this beautiful young lady, I called out to God in a drunken haze. Although I did not quite understand it, I had heard this could be done in my state. At the time I did not know why I did it, but I knew I was fed up with my life. I was barely getting by in college and I had actually considered dropping out if I could find a full-time job. That night as I was lying in bed something (or as I later found out Someone) had gotten to me. I had no dreams and no aspirations. Basketball was long gone and I had no idea where I wanted to go in life.

I will never forget that evening. For some reason, I was lonely. I was surrounded by friends, but I was lonely. I needed companionship so I began to describe my perfect woman to God, in detail. I have always had a great imagination. I had a picture of her in my head. That night, with the bed still spinning, I fell into unconsciousness and I did not think much more about it…for about a year.

To my utter amazement, and it took quite some time to realize it, God not only heard my prayer, but within two weeks He had answered it! What still amazes me today is *how* He answered it. He chose this strong little Asian girl from a far-away land who was as different as one could possibly be from me, both physically and spiritually. He literally sent her from halfway around the world and she put an end to my partying. To this day, I still do not know how, and at the time I had no idea that I was on the verge of encountering what I now regard to be God culture.

Once my head cleared, I began to see again and I began the long journey that brought me all the way to the place I am today. This was the time when my hunger for and my life-long pursuit of the Almighty began. There was no mistaking that God had answered my prayer, and what I have recently discovered twenty-one years later is that He did not leave out one little detail. I am utterly convinced that if you call out to Him, He will do the same for you. I am no one special. I also know how confusing and even awkward it feels to call out to Him after so many years of not realizing He has been an integral part of your life.

That fateful night while lying there in bed, I began to search…and six years later I found Him: Jesus Christ of Nazareth, the Lamb of God who takes away the sin of the world. He is the great Physician who heals the brokenhearted and restores broken lives and shattered dreams.

It was not long before I began to realize that most people were just like me and have a stark misconception of who God actually is, how He operates, and how one can get to know Him in a personal way. As I began discovering some of His "mysteries," people began to ask me questions. To my utter amazement, I could actually answer them.

However, the one question that is so elusive and so incredibly common throughout the ages has been and always will be, "How do you know?" My friend, this is not a particularly easy question to answer and it cannot be answered in one sentence or even one paragraph. So I began writing, never really intending for it to be published. I wrote it for me with the intention of one day passing it on to my children. It was to be my legacy. At least that was my original plan.

What you are about to read is a compilation of the things I have learned over the years, carefully woven together with the personal revelations that God has disclosed to me. What I once thought was intended just for me, I have now realized has been purposed for you all along. You will soon learn that this is a major aspect of God culture. God culture does not allow such vital information to be kept to oneself. Do not believe for a minute that this is just some random book by some random author and that you picked it up by accident. This is a "God thing."

That is my hope—that as you read through the rest of this book, and through the series, you will begin to gain an understanding of who God is and how He is working *with* you and *for* you through the trials and tribulations that every man and woman must experience in life. Even more importantly, as you begin to gain this understanding, I hope you will come to understand God's ultimate plan for your life: the salvation of your soul.

The Purpose of the Understanding the Almighty Series

The purpose of this book series is to invite you to understand God's overall plan within the workings of your everyday life, especially during your times of greatest trial. God does not think like a man. His wisdom and knowledge is infinitely greater than ours, and His will is for you to prosper and grow even when life seems unbearable.

God always sees life from this perspective and, without the proper understanding you may become either hopeless or deceived. This confusion has caused many to drift away from God, and for what even might seem to be good reason. When we see our lives through the eyes of Yahweh and gain clarity, we quickly learn that God has an incredible ability to harmoniously bind every situation together for the good of every individual and, ultimately, for the good of mankind as a whole.

We live in the here and now. For many of us, the future consists of what we will do later today or tomorrow, or perhaps even a week, a month, and maybe even a year from now. A person of great vision may think about the next three, five, ten or twenty years. But with God, "...*One day is as a thousand years, and a thousand years is as one day.*" (2 Peter 3:8)

Unlike us, God is not constrained by time. Nor is He bound by it, nor to it. Days, weeks, months, and even years are but a "flash" in eternity. In eternity, time is irrelevant. Everything just is. In the natural realm, He has a majestic ability to transcend space and time. While you are only able to see one word on a page, God is able to see the entire book plus all of its sequels in a mere moment.

As a result, He operates from the standpoint of foresight. We do not have the same gift of perspective; therefore His ways seem to be mysterious. However, you will no longer be bound by the trials of life and the uncertainty of wondering why things happen the way they do when you absorb and reflect upon the discussions in this book. My intention is to help you begin to see them as the opportunities they truly are.

"It is only in misery that we recognize
the hand of God leading good men to good."
—Johann Wolfgang von Goethe

When properly understood, trouble will no longer bind you; it will set you free. You will cease to be a slave to your greatest and sometimes innermost trepidations, and your fear will be replaced with triumph.

Starting with the first chapter, you will begin a journey that will unlock the unsearchable riches of God Almighty. The mysteries of life, death and religion are at your fingertips.

Sit back and relax, as you are about to voyage into the unknown. Waiting for you within the pages of this book is the key to unlocking the mystery of living your most extraordinary life. It is the knowledge of the Almighty Ancient of Days, and it is my privilege to introduce you to the God of the Universe. It is my pleasure to bring to you *The Understanding the Almighty Series*. As opposed to the pop culture that is so prevalent in the media today, you are about to experience *God Culture*. If you dare to apply this knowledge, your life will never be the same again.

— CHAPTER 1 —

Now vs. Forever

O ver the years, I have become utterly convinced that humanity spends way too much time fixating on the "now" and, as a result, we have very little understanding of what the "forever" is all about. Allow me to explain. An immense amount of focus both in and out of the church has been placed upon earthly success—in particular, financial success. Don't get me wrong. I believe wholeheartedly in striving to optimize the gifts God has endowed each and every individual with, and I believe in being successful.

For many people, however, success—in particular financial success—breeds failure, primarily when it is garnered quickly and conspicuously. Although this may sound strange upon you first hearing it, the evening news as well as the tabloids proves this sad truth on a daily basis. We sit back and wonder, "How can someone be so miserable and out of control when the entire world is at their fingertips?"

What many do not understand is that "the world" and its expectations are exactly the problem. When our entire notion of success is based upon how much money and prestige one has, what do you do when you arrive there? With this misguided understanding of self-worth and purpose, one can easily reach the pinnacle of their life in their low to mid-twenties, or even earlier. Then the real problems begin: boredom, too much time, a lack of meaningful purpose, and a deepening sense of emptiness that must be filled.

With no spiritual foundation, Lucifer and perhaps even more common, *you,* will be more than happy to fill the void with alcohol, drugs, sex, "partying" or whatever self-indulgent pleasure your twisted mind can conceive. Yet, this perceived "happiness" is temporary. It can only last as long as the self-induced numbness does before it wears off and returns you to your previous hangover of emptiness, which slowly emerges into the painful spiral of self-destruction and darkness. I know this because I have been there. I have danced with the devil and, trust me, you will never be the one to lead.

So what is the solution to this problem? We must learn to redefine success. We must redefine our culture. Success does not only pertain to finances, but to every area of your life, spirit, soul and body. Therefore, we must change our culture from "pop" to God.

There must be an experience of "salvation" on both a personal and cultural level. The very word that translates into "salvation" comes from the Greek word "soteria." We have been misled about its true meaning throughout our entire lives. Soteria does not just mean that you have been saved spiritually and that you are going to heaven. Along with your spiritual salvation, soteria also means you have been "saved" in every aspect of your life. You have been delivered from fear, self-loathing, inadequacy, or whatever your particular complication may be. You are no longer broken.

Think seriously about it for a moment. If you are rich yet too sick to enjoy it due to the abuse of your physical body, are you really successful? How about if your family is a mess, which is the case for many families throughout the world regardless of social status? Doesn't the same hold true regarding our culture? Is there any real success in broken marriages and raising rebellious children?

We continually hear of divorce settlements in the millions "these days," but the truth is these folks are not successful. They are utter failures caught in the middle of a failing culture. Are they wealthy? Yes. Successful? No. I am not saying that you cannot move on and become successful, but you will not unless you change the underlying cause of what bred those failures to begin with. Otherwise, like a broken record, the vicious cycle continuously repeats itself.

If you are considered by "the world" as the greatest human being who ever lived and you die and go to hell, were you a success? How about if your family follows you into the fire? Are you successful? Obviously the answer is no. We must learn to change our perception from immediate gratification to meaning and purpose. In my opinion, that can only be found in Christ. Christ is the solution. He is our strength and the rock of our salvation, personally and culturally.

With all that I have said thus far, please understand that prosperity is imperative to the success of the work of the body of Christ. In order to put that particular aspect of the Word of God into its proper perspective, we must have an understanding of the "forever." Most of us will live 70, 80, or perhaps even 90 years in the "now" on this planet.

If we have Christ, we will spend eternity in the "forever." This is why we must learn to worship, pray, hear and respond to God's direction. In fact, all of these disciplines that are practiced in the "now" are designed to bridge the gap to "forever." If that is true, shouldn't the rest of our lives reflect the same purpose?

Before we move forward, allow me to correct a previous statement. I heretofore indicated that if you have Christ, you will spend eternity in the "forever." The reality is that whether you have Christ or not, you will spend eternity in the "forever," but where will your "forever" be? That is the ninety-nine thousand dollar question. Will it be in heaven with the Lord or in hell with the devil and his fallen angels?

Obedience to Christ, who commanded us to make disciples of all nations, is to change a person's eternal destination from hell to heaven.

Unless you have an understanding of the "forever" and the finality and potential horror of it, you will not have the motivation to rescue those around you.

The New Gospel

Unfortunately, humanity has begun to experience a selfish gospel. For many of us, our prayer lives have become nothing more than, "Lord save me, make me rich and then I'll do something for You." The problem is that God is not *required* to do *anything* for us. He is not even required to save us. God does as He pleases, and it pleases Him to help us. It pleases Him to save us, and it pleases Him to give us His kingdom. (Luke 12:32) This is a direct result of His love, grace and mercy toward us. It is not about instant gratification. It is about your development as a human being and as a person of God.

There are times when we are required to experience certain trials to inherit His kingdom. I think we have been given the wrong idea about how this is accomplished. When you examine the Word of God carefully, every prophet including Jesus Himself experienced great trials. It is a part of Jewish culture.

The prophets of old were not just instantaneously given the kingdom of God. The process requires time, patience and perseverance, and just like God did not leave them, He has not left us during our times of trial and tribulation either. Deep within our troubles, God has a specific guiding purpose in mind and, more often than not, we are momentarily unable to comprehend His will through the chaos.

In believing that trouble is outside of God's plan, we have blotted out an important aspect of the Word of God. As a result, when trials and tribulations arise, we have been left naked and destitute of true understanding. I know that is not the intention of the "modern" message, but this is how it is being applied. This modernization of the Gospel leaves us immature and without understanding.

Former United States President Calvin Coolidge said, "It is only when men begin to worship that they begin to grow." It has been my experience that most people have not spent the proper time studying, praying and especially *doing* the Word of God to truly gain the proper perspective in regard to discerning God's will for their life. This immaturity is producing an "all about me" or an "all about *my church only*" gospel. Much like high school may have left some of you feeling, many churches have become nothing more than cliquish social clubs and its members have become ineffective and divided as a result.

My Way or the Highway

Think about it: What is the purpose of denomination? Isn't it to separate one church from the other based upon doctrinal differences? Denomination, which is defined in the Bible as sectarianism and clearly labeled as sin, is undoubtedly against the Word of God. Yet we have countless denominations, and the majority of them continue to move further from the Word of God, not closer.

The truth and beauty of God is that He loves every human being equally, regardless of race, religion and/or sexual preference, and He is inviting all of us to be a part of eternity with Him. Humanity as a whole is flawed and, as you read through this book, you will realize that the most imperfect member of all is me. Please do not misconstrue the following comment as gay bashing or any form of hatred intended to exclude any one group of people from the love of God. It is merely intended to illustrate how being disobedient to the Word of God causes us to become separated from both God and man.

The introduction of homosexual and lesbian Pastors, as controversial as it may be, is a clear example of societal pressures perverting the nature of God's Word. This, along with *all* sexual sin, is a reproach within the Word of God. Although it does not prohibit one from being part of the church, it does preclude one from having a position of leadership within the church.

Yet it has become a debate and a practice within several "mainline" denominations. The result of this has not been to unite but to further divide the people of God. Any and all rebellion against God and His

Word will always produce the same outcome. It is a direct result of living "now" vs. "forever." This is a prime example of how pop culture is in direct conflict with God culture.

Modern human beings want their way, and they want it now. We rarely consider who else may be affected by our actions. This "now" mentality will cause countless millions to suffer in the "forever." This may also be true of our "modern day Christianity," if the goal of the individual becomes the never-ending search for riches and prideful pleasure in lieu of the will of God. It is a satanic perversion. *"For what profit is it to a man if he gains the whole world but loses his own soul."* (Matthew 16:26)

Let's begin to change our focus to what is truly important. If we *"seek first the kingdom of God and His righteousness* (if we seek the forever) *all these things* (in the now) *will be added to you."* (Matthew 6:33) It is only with an understanding of the "forever" that the "now" will not be distorted, and it is only with an understanding of the "forever" that the "now" can even be truly understood. Proverbs 4:7 states that wisdom should be the primary focus of our desires, for it brings with it understanding. It is my opinion that both spiritual and physical prosperity result from each individual understanding the true will of God for their life.

If you are ready and willing, and please know that God is offering, the following chapters are about to introduce you to the *"the mind of Christ"* (1 Corinthians 2:16) and the true will of God.

Let's begin our journey…

— CHAPTER 2 —

Foresight's 20/20

I once heard it said, "Life can only be truly understood when looking backward." It took me quite a while not just to process how accurate this is but to actually accept it as truth. From the standpoint of man, I believe this to be absolutely valid. We cannot predict or knowingly change the future—only God can.

God never looks backward. Every intervention He has ever had with mankind is to bring His will to pass either now or at some point in the future. Every prophecy He has ever disclosed to man is forward-looking. It is part of what makes Him divine. This is what makes me so confident in believing the old cliché that, "God is in control." He actually is.

God meticulously determines the time, place, players and nature of each event that takes place. To see this point in action, I would like to lead you through the amazing, and what some may even consider tragic, events that transpired in the life of Joseph, the son of Jacob who bore the nation of Israel.

Revenge Is Sweet

> *"Now Israel loved Joseph more than all his children*
> *because he was the son of his old age."*
> **—Genesis 37:3**

As many of you already know, favoritism can be the cause of multiple problems ranging from jealousy to a lack of self-esteem and all the way to crimes as extreme as murder. Ancient societies placed the majority of the favor upon the firstborn son. He was to receive the greater portion of the inheritance as well as the blessing. When God wanted to show His immense power to Pharaoh by plaguing Egypt in the days of Moses, what was His grand finale? It was the death of the firstborn in all of Egypt.

Even today, the firstborn son can be the source of a man's greatest pride. Yet Israel's favorite was his youngest son in a society devoid of political correctness and the knowledge of one's psychological makeup. Imagine the hurt and jealousy this would have caused Joseph's brothers to feel. As you will find out shortly, they had no intention of hiding it.

> *"Also, he made him a tunic of many colors. But when his brothers*
> *saw that their father loved him more than all his other brothers, they*
> *hated him and could not speak peaceably to him. Now Joseph had a*
> *dream, and he told it to his brothers, and they hated him even more."*
> **—Genesis 37:3-5**

To make matters worse, Joseph has a dream that predicts he will rule over his older brothers. We do not know if Joseph was being braggadocios or naïve when he decided to disclose his dream to them. The Bible does not tell us his motivation, but I have an inkling that it may have been a little bit of both. Joseph was immature and it was no secret who his father favored. Needless to say, this did not sit very well with the other eleven brothers.

Keep in mind that we have watched this scene be perpetually played out over the course of history as God's chosen people, or to use the vernacular of this theme—God's favorite people, have been continuously persecuted throughout history. The following is merely a foreshadowing of the horrendous events to be perpetuated against Israel in the millennia to come.

With regard to Joseph, however, who could have ever imagined what was about to transpire between him and his brothers? Certainly Joseph couldn't. (For more on the dream refer to Genesis 37.)

"Then his brothers went to feed his father's flock in Shechem. And Israel said to Joseph, 'Are not your brothers feeding the flock in Shechem? Come, I will send you to them… Now when they saw him afar off, even before he came near them, they conspired against him to kill him… But Reuben heard it and delivered him out of their hands, and said, 'Let us not kill him.' And Reuben said to them, 'Shed no blood, but cast him into this pit which is in the wilderness, and do not lay a hand on him,'—that he might deliver him out of their hands, and bring him back to their father… Then they took him and cast him into a pit… And they sat down to eat a meal."

"Then they lifted their eyes and looked, and there was a company of Ishmaelites, coming from Gilead to feed their camels… So Judah said to his brothers, 'What profit is there if we kill our brother and conceal his blood? Come let us sell him to the Ishmaelites. (Ishmaelites are the sons of Ishmael which constitute the Arab nations of today) *And let not our hand be upon him'…"*

"So the brothers lifted Joseph up out of the pit, and sold him to the Ishmaelites for twenty shekels of silver. And they took Joseph to Egypt… Then Reuben returned to the pit (he must not have been present for the sale), *and indeed Joseph was not in the pit, and he tore his clothes* (I can only imagine the panic he must have felt)… *Now the Midianites* (Ishmaelites) *had sold him to Egypt to Potiphar, an officer of Pharaoh and Captain of the Guard."*

—Genesis 37:12-36

Let me stop this popular story from the Scriptures at this point, as I would like to begin discussing the perfect will and plan of God. To begin, please allow me to ask a question: What do you think was going through the mind of Joseph? We know the end of the story, but Joseph did not. It is easy for us to just dismiss this event as being under God's control.

We seem to have this idea that Joseph is standing around like Flounder, the character from the movie *Animal House*, and thinking, "Boy, this is *great*! I'm definitely in God's will now." No way, man! If anything, he is thinking, "Lord, what about that dream you gave me, remember? The one where my family was bowing before me? My own *brothers* just considered killing me and have now sold me into slavery to a bunch of savages." Joseph must be thinking, "I'm finished. Dead! It can't possibly get any worse than this."

As we are about to find out…not only can it, but it is about to get immeasurably worse for Joseph. Joseph will find out God's will later and he will certainly look back with an understanding of God's overall plan; however, at this point in the story, Joseph is scared and probably in shock. Things are looking bleak. He has got to be angry and confused. Have you ever felt this way about something that has happened in your life? Perhaps you even blamed God for your trouble. I am sure Joseph was tempted to do the same. Let's continue on…

"Now Joseph had been taken down to Egypt…"

We will find out shortly that, unbeknownst to Joseph, God placed him *exactly* where He wanted him. It is imperative that we learn to recognize this in our own lives. If you obey Him, God will guide you to the exact place you need to be in order to accomplish *His* will for your life. In most cases, He will present you with a choice and be patient enough for you to recognize His will. Once you do, you must be obedient to it.

Under certain circumstances, however, God must actually remove you from one place, perhaps a job, city, etc., and *place* you where He needs you to be—and oftentimes by any means necessary. Joseph's life is an illustration of one of these unusual circumstances because the situation about to develop will affect countless millions and, in fact, billions of people throughout history.

Therefore, God needed to move Joseph out of harm's way. There was no room for Joseph to choose. At first glance, it appears that God may have failed in His efforts as Joseph finds himself in an extremely perilous situation, but in God culture things are not always as they appear. Almighty God possessed the foresight to remedy the eternal situation that was about to unfold.

> *"Now Joseph had been taken down to Egypt. And Potiphar, an officer of Pharaoh, and captain of the guard, an Egyptian, bought him from the Ishmaelites who had taken him down there.* ***The Lord was with Joseph, and he was a successful man,*** *and he was in the house of his master the Egyptian.* ***And his master saw that the Lord was with him and that the Lord made all he did prosper in his hand.*** *So Joseph found favor in his sight and served him. Then he made him overseer of his house, and all that he had, he put under his authority. So it was from the time he made him overseer of his house and all that he had,* ***that the Lord blessed the Egyptian's house for Joseph's sake; and the blessing of the Lord was on all that he had in the house and in the field.*** *Thus he left all that he had in Joseph's hand, and he did not know what he had except for the bread that he ate."*
> **—Genesis 39:1-6**

If you did not pay attention to the Scriptures above, read them again. You will find a tremendous spiritual message within these six verses of Scripture.

First and foremost, take note of the fact that God was able to prosper Joseph in what appears to be a horrendous situation. Joseph has now gone from a prosperous free man, from a supremely prominent family, to a slave, the lowest of the low. In terms of social status, slavery is as far down the ladder as you can possibly fall.

God does not care about your social status. Material possessions are irrelevant in God culture. He does not care what your "name" is. God can prosper you anywhere, anytime, and under any circumstance. God is now prospering Joseph to the point that his master Potiphar begins to notice.

What I find extremely interesting is the fact that the Scripture states in verse 2 that Joseph was a "successful man." Well, how can a *slave* be successful? There is no upward mobility in that profession. Heck, you don't even get paid. My only explanation is that when God is with you, no matter what your situation, *you are successful!* Notice I did not say you *will be* successful. I said you *are* successful. You cannot fail because He cannot fail.

There are several areas of success to consider in all this. The majority of a man's success has very little to do with money. Most importantly, consider acknowledging that God is the most valuable asset that you can possibly possess. Without Him, you can do nothing of lasting worth. In fact, without Him you are nothing. You have no worth. You are just a walking pile of "stuff" that will merely decompose into dirt upon your last breath. You cannot be saved; and by the way, you cannot even breathe without Him.

Salvation, which we defined earlier, however, is the ultimate success. It allows you to spend eternity with God. Although true salvation *does* leave room for earthly success, in eternity you will have no need of your so-called "accomplishments." They all belong to the Lord anyway.

In addition to this, it is important to recognize that *everything* God comes in contact with prospers. Everything! —Unless it is for judgment. Even judgment, however, leads to the prosperity of the righteous. Righteousness is defined as those who are in right standing with God, and it can only be found in Christ who reunites you to the Father.

When you have God, you have love, peace, joy, wisdom, power, patience and blessing—no matter where you are, who you are with, or what the circumstance is. That is the true definition of success, and it is the essence of God culture. That is a success that no man can take from you. You can take a man's money from him. You can take his home, his pride, or any number of possessions, but you can never take a man's blessing. The blessing is God's to give and yours to throw away through ignorance or, perhaps even, conscious disobedience.

What Do *You* See?

Now understand, God will not revoke the plan He has for your life, but you can separate yourself from it and Him through sin, ignorance and disobedience. Once you repent, however, you can be fully restored to fellowship. It is as if you are just like a child who disobeys his parents, knowingly or unknowingly, so you will need to work to regain your Father's trust.

If you could only seek one thing in life, what would it be? Riches, fame, honor, you name it. I would strongly suggest that the primary object of your affection be the diligent pursuit of Almighty God, His Spirit, and the infilling thereof. With the Creator of all that exists residing within you, with all His wisdom, it is impossible to fail. Why would you desire anything else? I must warn you though: as you mature, God will change your definition of success and rightly so. You will move from the material to the spiritual. This is confirmation that you are entering God culture and only then can God work fully through you.

If God is truly with you, people will most likely notice. When Joseph showed up in Egypt, so did Yahweh. The beauty of God culture is that it is contagious. When it is genuine, it affects everyone around you. Not only did Joseph prosper, but Potiphar began to experience a success that he was unable to comprehend. His only explanation was what he saw. The great I AM was with Joseph. As a result, Joseph's blessing was upon Potiphar and his whole household as well. This was recognized by an unbelieving, heretofore polytheistic, Egyptian heathen. Guess what? If God was seen in Joseph, He can be seen in you as well.

We have all had situations in our lives where things just seem to go right. We cannot explain them or put our fingers on why. They just do. The situation with Joseph and Potiphar was beyond going right. It was *supernatural*. It was inexplicable in human terms. It can only be explained as God culture. Everything Joseph touched turned to gold, and Potiphar knew it. Joseph was so full of the Almighty that when Potiphar looked at Joseph, he saw God. Therefore, he entrusted Joseph with everything he had.

How about you, can your boss trust you in the same way? Can your boss see God in you the way Potiphar saw God in Joseph?

How about your friends and family, do they see God in you? How wonderful it would be if the unsaved of the world could see God clearly in us. The truth is that most of us walk so close to the edge of righteousness that folks just don't notice. *They see us in us, but not God in us.* As a result, we all suffer. Through ignorance, apathy or just plain disobedience you are separated from God's blessing and favor. The resulting chaos extinguishes the power of God in our lives and eradicates our ability to participate and fulfill His eternal plan. Consequently the people you influence on a day-to-day basis never get introduced to the one and only true God and, pop culture has its way with them.

God Minded

Joseph was different than most people. He had a different outlook on life. When faced with adversity, Joseph refused to compromise both *his* integrity *and* God's integrity. Take a look at the following Scriptures.

> *"Now Joseph was handsome in form and appearance and it came to pass after these things that his master's wife cast longing eyes on Joseph, and she said, 'Lie with me.' But he refused and said to his masters' wife, 'Look, my master does not know what is with me in the house, and has committed all that he has to my hand. There is no one greater in this house than I, nor has he kept anything back from me **but you,** because you are his wife. How then can I do this great wickedness, **and sin against God?'** So it was, as she spoke to Joseph **day by day,** that **he did not heed her,** to lie with her or to be with her."*
> **—Genesis 39:6-9**

What made Joseph different? A man such as Potiphar would not have had an ugly wife. A man in his position had choices. Potiphar's wife must have been beautiful. He was a man of great power. There was no "women's lib" movement back then. Women did not have rights as they do today. Marriage was their upward mobility. It could change the legacy of an entire lineage of people. Therefore, not just women, but entire families would have been pursuing Potiphar to offer their most prized possessions, their beautiful daughters, to him.

Let this be a warning. The presence of God in you makes you attractive. Not in a physical sense, but in a spiritual sense. While Potiphar understood the source of Joseph's greatness, his wife did not. She saw something in Joseph that she wanted. She knew he was different, but she did not recognize the source of Joseph's attractiveness.

It was not just that Joseph was handsome. There was something more to Joseph, something beyond his physical appearance that actually made him irresistible. Many a man of God has fallen as a result of this. Do not allow yourself to be next.

Take a good look at this situation. Potiphar's wife was an aristocrat. These folks did not intermingle with "the help," yet she could not keep her hands off the Hebrew slave. Joseph endured these seductions day in and day out; but Joseph had something that we do not see very often in the world today. Joseph had loyalty. Joseph had integrity. Joseph was faithful and truly cared about his boss, Potiphar.

Joseph was well-versed in the God culture passed down from his father, Jacob, and, unlike his brothers, Joseph put it into practice. This seemingly simple lifestyle unleashed the power of God in Joseph's life that delivered and prospered him, regardless of circumstance. Wouldn't you love to know God in this intimate way? You can, and you will, if you are willing to make one minor, but significant lifestyle shift that makes God culture *your* culture.

If you think logically about it, don't you think Joseph's attributes make perfect sense? How could a man of God such as Joseph be any other way? He had been transformed into the image of God. His day-to-day contact and intimate relationship with God Almighty is what gave him the strength to endure his master's wife's incessant requests.

We do not see this type of leadership in our world today. Does Hollywood produce it in the films and television shows we watch? How about in those we elect to represent us in the United States Senate or House of Representatives? What about in the business world? What we see more often in our world today is licentious, which is immoral behavior with no sense of self-control, infidelity and unfaithfulness. We mostly see "now only" living, which has produced a culture that ignores, or perhaps even denies the existence of God and His Spirit.

So what are we receiving in return? All too often we simply accept a culture of sin, which we unwittingly consent to without even questioning the potential consequence to the world around us. This, unfortunately, produces spiritual death and a society that continues to degrade. By simply focusing on the "now" we are cutting off the "forever."

There *is* another way. Let's look at integrity and righteousness, which produces life. Let's learn God culture! Watch how Joseph replies to these sexual advances.

> *"How can I do this great wickedness and sin against God?"*
> **—Genesis 39:9**

When Joseph was tempted with sin, he did not focus on it. It was never even a possibility in his mind because his focus was firmly on God. If you look back upon the life of his father, Jacob, and his grandfather, Isaac, you will soon realize that this was the culture Joseph was brought up in. Joseph was "God-minded." He grew up in God culture.

I find it interesting that Joseph did not consider this great wickedness to be against Potiphar, even though it was Potiphar's wife. He considered this great wickedness to be against God Almighty. (We find this same attitude in King David. David, with all of his faults and shortcomings, was considered a friend of God, a man after God's own heart.)

So what is it that stops *you* from acting upon temptation? Is it your love for God? Is it your integrity, or are you afraid your husband or wife may find out? We must develop this same love of God like Joseph. Joseph equated betraying *the heathen Egyptian* Potiphar with betrayal of God.

Can you imagine? Joseph equated his *slave master* with the King of the universe! Joseph and Potiphar had nothing in common. They were not the same race or religion. Yet Joseph still respected Potiphar. In addition, although being treated fairly well, Joseph was being held against his will.

How could he feel this way? The answer is perseverance. As a result of his life experience and the tribulations he endured, Joseph had a different understanding of God than most other people. Joseph realized that God actually loved Potiphar as much as God loved him.

Do not forget that Joseph understood betrayal. He experienced it firsthand. His brothers betrayed him. Joseph also must have understood how his brother's acts of betrayal hurt Israel (Jacob), his father, who believed he lost a beloved child as a result. It was not only Joseph who was betrayed by the horrific acts of his eleven brothers; Israel was betrayed as well. He lost his beloved son. Joseph was not going to betray God, his heavenly Father, in the same way.

Do not believe for one second that Joseph was not tempted by Potiphar's beautiful wife. I'll bet there were days, and perhaps even nights, when Joseph was close to breaking, but he stayed intimately close to God—and God delivered him from evil. That is why we say in the "Our Father" prayer, "...*lead us not into temptation, but deliver us from evil.*" That is why we pray any prayer for that matter. You must nurture your relationship with God, just as you would nurture your marriage. In order to cohabitate with Him, and invite Him to be the central figure in your life, you must learn His culture and learn to love and live with Him.

From Bad to Worse

As we return to Scripture, things are about to turn ugly for Joseph. He is about to experience more injustice, tribulation and persecution. Is it God's will, or has Satan taken over the situation? Let's learn to read and review the Scriptures from a new perspective and create a new experience of understanding and discernment. Things are about to go from not so bad to horrific for Joseph. How will he react? How would *you* react? Let's draw wisdom from Joseph, one of the greatest prophets the world has ever known.

*"But it happened about this time, when Joseph went into the house to do his work, **and none of the men of the house were inside,** that*

she caught him by his garment saying, 'Lie with me.' But he left his garment in her hand and fled and ran outside. And so it was, when she saw that he had left his garment and ran outside, that she called to the men of the house and spoke to them, saying, 'See, he has brought in to us a Hebrew to mock us. (This statement is important. She has positioned herself against her husband and is attempting to turn the household as well.) *He came in to me to lie with me, and I cried out with a loud voice. And it happened, when he heard that I lifted my voice and cried out, that he left his garment with me and fled outside."*

"*So she kept his garment with her until the master came home. Then she spoke to him with words **like these**, saying, 'The Hebrew servant **that you brought to us** came in to me to mock me; so it happened, as I lifted my voice and cried out, that he left his garment with me and fled outside."*

"*So it was, when his master heard the words which his wife spoke to him saying, 'your servant did to me after this manner,' that his anger was aroused. Then Joseph's master took him and put him into the prison, **a place where the king's prisoners were confined**. And he was there in the prison."*

—Genesis 39:11-20

What just happened? At this point Joseph must think he is cursed. We come to that conclusion in our own lives for a heck of a lot less. Just as Joseph's life was becoming bearable his master's wife attempts to seduce him. When things go awry and she is on the verge of being caught she blames Joseph and lies her way out of trouble. She got herself into a difficult situation and her first and only thought centered upon self-preservation. Think about what happened. She grabbed hold of Joseph, and as she pulled him near to her, his resistance caused his garment to come off. Joseph, recognizing the mess he was in, immediately fled the scene.

How is she to explain being in possession of Joseph's garment to her husband and his running through the courtyard naked or nearly so? Not only would she be humiliated by her infidelity, as would be her husband's name, but with a Hebrew *slave* of all people! She would be finished. She would have found herself in the same place Joseph was about to be sent. So what does she do? She cries, "**Rape!**" and lies in order to alter the truth regarding her own iniquity. If you see yourself in this scenario, I would simply encourage you to change your culture. Learn the will and ways of God. His nature will inevitably change yours, and you will be restored into His image.

Caught in the Middle

What no one considers is that this put Potiphar in a bad situation as well. The Scripture says Potiphar's anger was aroused when he heard the words of his wife, but I am not sure whom he was actually irritated with. We automatically make an assumption that he was angry with Joseph, because he put him in jail, but the Scripture does not actually say with whom he was angry.

Perhaps this was not the first time his wife's infidelity was an issue. She certainly had a major character flaw, and we see her immediately set herself against Potiphar, her husband. I would not be a bit surprised if her daily pursuit of Joseph was not the talk of the house, which by way of rumor would have most certainly made its way back to Potiphar.

Other envious and ambitious servants bidding for Joseph's position, and who quite possibly saw him naked and fleeing the house, would undoubtedly have used this situation as an attempt to rid themselves of Joseph the Hebrew, whom the Egyptians hated and considered to be beneath them. Interestingly enough, it seems that Potiphar did not want to have any part of what he knew was not Joseph's doing.

Remember, Potiphar knew that God was with Joseph and that Joseph was a man of utmost integrity. Also keep in mind that Potiphar is benefiting tremendously from this arrangement of having Joseph in his house. Joseph is multiplying Potiphar's wealth and his favor within the kingdom of Egypt on a daily basis. Potiphar is no dummy. No man prone to deception achieves his level of governmental rule. Potiphar would not entrust all he had to just anyone. He knew Joseph and absolutely trusted him. This situation does not make sense. So who was it that Potiphar was truly angry with?

A Win-Win Situation

I can only imagine Potiphar's reaction when he heard the news. "You've got to be kidding!" must have been his cry of frustration, but this dilemma left Potiphar in a "no win" situation. If he tells the truth, he risks embarrassment and humiliation. After all, she *is* his wife. If he does nothing, and chooses the Hebrew's word over his wife's word, he also becomes a societal outcast–most likely losing all he has. His only choice: put Joseph in prison, but Potiphar is slick. He did not choose just any prison. Remember, Potiphar is the captain of the guard. He chose the king's prison, which happens to be *his* dungeon located on *his* premises. This way he can monitor the situation and maybe still be attached to the blessing that came along with his most prized possession, Joseph.

Do not forget that God knows exactly what is happening here. Through all of this chaos and turmoil, He has a "forever" purpose in mind. Not only does God know what's happening, He is controlling every detail of the situation. God *needed* Joseph in prison at this point in human history. Joseph does not yet know why, Potiphar does not know why, and Pharaoh certainly does not know why…but a life and death battle, both in the spiritual and natural realms, is about to arise which requires Joseph to be imprisoned.

God's wisdom, power, and ability to control every situation simultaneously are unparalleled in the universe, and His ways are most certainly not our ways. You will thank God for this in a moment, once you truly understand what is happening in this story, which even affects your own present day life.

The Right Man

Although God always has a "forever" plan, He also knows that you have a "now" need. He knew that Joseph had a "now" need too. To function properly in your natural and spiritual life, you must grasp the following principle: *"No temptation has overtaken you except such is common to man;*

but God is faithful, who will not allow you to be tempted beyond what you are able, but with the temptation will also make the way of escape, that you may be able to bear it." (1 Corinthians 10:13)

God did not just thrust any old human into Potiphar's house to be tempted by his beautiful wife. He sent Joseph. There is a reason that he did not send Judah or any of the other brothers. (Read the story of Judah and Tamar in Genesis 38 and you will understand why it was Joseph who had to go. Judah most likely would have been in that bed with Potiphar's wife in an instant, making an utter mess of God's eternal plan.)

God knew Joseph's character as well as his destiny. He knew Joseph would not give in, and He knew that Potiphar's wife would cry rape. He knew Joseph was about to be thrown into prison, and He knew Joseph could handle the hardship. Nevertheless, God is faithful. He knew what Joseph needed in prison and He was there to provide it. Let's examine Joseph's prison life.

Prosperity in Prison

*"**But the Lord was with Joseph and showed him mercy,** and He gave him favor in the sight of the keeper of the prison. And the keeper of the prison committed to Joseph's hand all the prisoners who were in the prison; whatever they did there, it was his doing. The keeper of the prison did not look into anything that was under Joseph's authority, **because the Lord was with him,** and whatever he did, the Lord made it prosper."*
—Genesis 39:21-23

We are beginning to see a recurring theme here. No matter what Joseph's situation is, God makes it prosper. Yes, Joseph was in prison, but he was running the place. However, not even Joseph had the foresight to recognize all that was happening at this point—even after experiencing God's favor in the house of Potiphar. God's plan is just too big.

Sometimes we read about our heroes in the Bible and forget that they are human with real fears, flaws, and anxieties. Joseph was not sinless and he was also not a superman. He was a man of integrity who fully trusted God with all of his heart and soul.

Do you actually believe that, while on his way to prison, Joseph was happy or fearless or whatever preconceived notion you may have? Let's be real. He was scared, angry and certainly frustrated. All he knew was (1) he was innocent and (2) that his life was about to change—and no doubt for the worse. Can you relate to this reaction? I have been scared, angry and frustrated over losing a job. I cannot even imagine the anxiety I would incur if I were being sent to prison, especially if I was wrongly convicted.

Let's look at the difference between Joseph's situation and many of our own. This is essential to being righteous, or in right relationship with God—for that is what righteousness means.

Unlike many of us, Joseph was innocent of the crime he was accused of committing. It is important to note that this is a Messianic parallel. Jesus was condemned and crucified while committing no crime. Yet just like Joseph was imprisoned, Jesus spent three days in Hades to pay the price for mankind's crime of sin.

For most people who have been imprisoned innocence is not the case. We are usually guilty and we must learn to discern the difference between God's will and our own stupidity. If I get thrown in jail for robbing a bank or drunk driving, that is stupidity. If I am enduring a situation not of my own doing, then something else could be going on.

Look Within Yourself

Examine yourself when you experience trials and tribulations. Ask yourself if you are the cause—and be honest. Is the problem a result of sin or bad habits? Are you sowing bad seeds and reaping a defiled harvest, or is something else going on? Perhaps you are being refined.

There is no such thing as luck, good or bad. Things primarily happen to us based upon the result of the choices we make on a daily basis. It is called the law of sowing and reaping.

Every once in a while, God needs to accomplish something on this earth and places us in a situation that we cannot seem to manage. Do not fear if this is you. God is always in control. "***His strength** is made* *perfect in **your weakness**,"* (2 Corinthians 12:9) and *"the foolishness of God is wiser than men, and the weakness of God is stronger than men."* (1 Corinthians 1:25)

This explains how we can *"rejoice, though now for a little while,* (Note that there should be a pause here; I believe the Scripture has been punctuated incorrectly by the translators as it contains two separate concepts that should be separated into two sentences.) **if need be**, *you have been grieved by various trials, that the genuineness of your faith, being more precious than gold that perishes, though it is tested by fire, may be found to praise, honor, and glory at the revelation of Jesus Christ, whom having not seen you love."* (1 Peter 1:6-8)

God needs to grieve us from time to time. If He does not, we simply get too "puffed up" and lose sight of Him. To our amazement, Christ is revealed in the midst of our trials.

Pure Gold

Without a "forever" mindset, you will find it impossible to rejoice when tested. After all, how can one rejoice when they are faced with a perceived harmful situation? That would be craziness. A man without God in his life, or a Christian without understanding, has no "forever" vision. They can only perceive the "now." The truth is: your life in the "now" is only temporary. These years in the natural realm are the equivalent of a fetus in the womb. As a fetus, you grow and strengthen and prepare to be birthed into the "world." However, just as in the natural realm, when your eventual time of delivery arrives, you will be birthed into eternity. Life is ultimately about the "forever."

To understand why we are tested, let's take a closer look at how gold was purified in ancient times. When gold comes out of the ground, it is not ready to be formed into a necklace or ring. It is mined in chunks of rock and dirt. The worthless substance commingled with the gold ore is called "dross."

In order to purify the gold, you must separate it from the dross. How is that done? It is refined with fire. As you heat it, the gold melts and separates from the dross. A substance called flux is then introduced into the mixture, and it draws all of the impurities to itself. Quite simply, the heavier more valuable substance sinks to the bottom of the pot and the impurities float and stick to the flux. You pour off the garbage and what you are left with is pure refined gold.

Have you ever considered Jesus to be your flux? When you invite Him into the mix, He draws all of your sin, sickness and iniquity to Him. Through His death and resurrection, He has poured it into the grave and left it in hell where it belongs. What is left is a pure undefiled man recreated into the image of God. Pure gold!

Obviously it is not physical fire that refines us. It is the holy fire of trials and tribulations that we endure throughout our lives. These coupled with filling ourselves with God's Word work together to perfect us and prepare us to face the even greater trials that await us throughout our natural lives. The refining process requires a certain amount of pain, or at least discomfort. There is a "forever" purpose within them. Your job is to discern that purpose and that usually takes time, patience and faith.

Let's return to our story. Joseph is about to be tested by fire throughout his prison sentence. We will soon find out God's "forever" plan for him.

Dream Weaver

We are now about to enter what I would refer to as the "dream phase" of Joseph's prison sentence. There will be no doubt to all those involved that God is on the scene. We will begin to see the "forever" plan of God unfold right before our very eyes. Take note, as God begins to reveal things, you will most likely only catch a "page" of God's plan. As we come to the end of this chapter, I hope to show you the entire "book."

> *"It came to pass after these things that the butler and the baker offended their lord* (Pharaoh), *the king of Egypt. And Pharaoh was angry with his two officers, the chief butler and the chief baker. So he put them in custody in the house of the captain of the guard,* (Which is who? That's right, Potiphar!) *in the prison, the place where Joseph was confined. And the captain of the guard charged Joseph with them, and he served them, so they were in custody for a while.*

"Then the butler and the baker of the king of Egypt, who were confined in the prison, had a dream, both of them, each man's dream in one night and each man's dream with its own interpretation. And Joseph came in to them in the morning and looked at them, and saw that they were sad. So he asked Pharaoh's officers who were with him in custody of his lord's house saying, 'Why do you look so sad today?'

*"And they said to him, 'We each have had a dream, and there is no interpreter of it.' So Joseph said to them, **'Do not interpretations belong to God? Tell them to me, please.'"***
—Genesis 40:1-8

There are two things we need to note here. First, Joseph was truly a caring and discerning man. You will always find this quality within those whom God culture resides. He immediately recognized that the butler and the baker were bothered by something. Remember: Joseph was in prison. Prison culture is not the friendliest place in the world, and most prisoners do not pay that close attention to nor care for one another enough to even notice if someone else is troubled. Joseph was not like these other men, which unfortunately he is about to find out firsthand.

Second, Joseph gave all the glory to God. It would have been very easy for Joseph to say, "*I* can interpret that dream, tell it to me." But he didn't. "I" was never Joseph's response. His response was always, "*God* can do it. Tell me your dream."

It's All About Me

What do you think was Satan's greatest sin? Check out Isaiah 14:12-15, *"How you have fallen from heaven, O Lucifer, son of the morning! You are cut down to the ground, you who weakened the nations! For you have said in your heart, "**I will** ascend into heaven. **I will** exalt **my throne** above the stars of God. **I will** also sit on the mount of the congregation on the farthest sides of the north. **I will** ascend above the heights of the clouds. **I will** be like the Most High.' **Yet you shall be brought down** to Sheol, to the lowest depths of the Pit."*

This is the exact opposite of Joseph's response. Joseph always remembered and glorified God for his success and/or abilities. Do you? We must learn to. Look at all of the "I will's" in Lucifer's discourse. Lucifer's greatest sin was **pride**. He could only obey *his own* will. Pride led him to self-exaltation and the execution of *his will* above God's will. We must learn to recognize when we are heading in this direction and cut it down immediately. Daniel 11:14, in the King James Version of the Bible, states, "… *the robbers of thy people shall exalt themselves… but they shall fall.*"

What is Lucifer? He is a thief and a robber. A robber is someone who steals by force as opposed to thievery, which may be done stealthily. Lucifer is both, and pride is the cause of his corruption. Lucifer's goal is to rob and steal God from your life. Will you let him? Will you allow pride to rule you? Pride and self-exaltation is the consummate counter to God culture. Lucifer has fallen, and so could you if you exalt *you* over God.

Joseph could have easily been bitter and blamed his problems on God. He could have moped around his whole time in Egypt, but he did not. He fully trusted God and kept Him close. Learn from this, and "… *humble yourselves under the mighty hand of God,* **that He may exalt you** *in due time, casting all your care upon Him,* **for He cares for you.**" (1 Peter 5:6) Joseph was a living example of this Scripture. Joseph exalted God, and in God's time God exalted Joseph. That is God culture. To experience true success, we must model our lives in like manner.

A Diamond in the Rough

> "*Then the chief butler told his dream to Joseph… And Joseph said to him, 'This is the interpretation of it: The three branches are three days. Now within three days Pharaoh will lift up your head and restore you to your place, and you will put Pharaoh's cup in his hand according to the former manner, when you were his butler.* **But remember me when it is well with you,** *and please show kindness to me, make mention of me to Pharaoh, and get me out of this house. For indeed I was stolen away from the hand of the Hebrews; and also I have done nothing here that they should put me*

into the dungeon.'" (Genesis 40:9-15) ***"Yet the chief butler did not remember Joseph,*** *but forgot him."*
—Genesis 40:23

And just like that, Joseph was left to rot in prison…

Remember Joseph's plea. It is very important to you seeing and understanding the "forever" plan of God regarding this story. In essence, Joseph was saying, "I'm innocent and I want to go home." Joseph was just a kid, seventeen or eighteen years old, when he arrived in Egypt. Imagine how homesick he must have felt, but, as I mentioned earlier, God needs Joseph to be in prison at this point in history. Going home is not an option. And here's why:

"Then it came to pass ***after two full years***, *that Pharaoh had a dream, and behold, he stood by the river…"* (Genesis 41:1) *"Now it came to pass in the morning that his* (Pharaoh's) *spirit was troubled, and he sent and called for all the magicians of Egypt and all its wise men… but there was no one who could interpret… Then the chief butler spoke to Pharaoh saying, 'I remember my faults this day. When Pharaoh was angry with his servants… we each had a dream in one night… Now there was a young Hebrew man with us there, a servant of the captain of the guard. And we told him and he interpreted our dreams for us…* ***And it came to pass***, *just as he interpreted for us, so it happened…' Then Pharaoh sent for Joseph…"*

"And Pharaoh said to Joseph, 'I have had a dream, and there is no one who can interpret it. But I have heard it said of you that you can understand a dream, to interpret it.' So Joseph answered Pharaoh, saying, ***'It is not in me, God will give Pharaoh an answer of peace.'"***
—Genesis 41:8-16

Once again we see Joseph's total and complete lack of self in his glorification of the Father. Pharaoh then explains the two dreams to Joseph and here is Joseph's interpretation:

"And Joseph said to Pharaoh, 'The dreams of Pharaoh are one; God has shown Pharaoh what He is about to do: the seven good cows are seven years, and the seven good heads are seven years; the dreams are one. And the seven thin and ugly cows which came up after them are seven years, and the seven empty heads blighted by the east wind are seven years of famine... Indeed seven years of great plenty will come all throughout the land of Egypt; but after them **seven years of famine will arise,** *and all the plenty will be forgotten in the land of Egypt,* **and the famine will deplete the land.** *So the plenty will not be known in the land because of the famine following,* **for it will be very severe...** *and God will bring it shortly to pass.'"*

"'Now therefore, let Pharaoh select a discerning and wise man, and set him over the land of Egypt. Let Pharaoh do this, and let him appoint officers over the land, to collect one fifth of the produce of the land of Egypt in the seven plentiful years... then that food shall be as a reserve for the land for the seven years of famine which shall be in the land of Egypt, **that the land may not perish during the famine.'"**

"So the advice was good in the eyes of Pharaoh and in the eyes of all his servants. And Pharaoh said to the servants, 'Can we find such a one as this, **a man in whom is the Spirit of God?'** *Then Pharaoh said to Joseph, 'Inasmuch as God has shown you all this, there is no one as wise and as discerning as you.* **You shall be over my house, and all my people shall be ruled according to your word; only in regard to the throne will I be greater than you.'** *And Pharaoh said to Joseph,* **'See, I have set you over all the land of Egypt.'"**

"Then Pharaoh took his signet ring off his hand and put it on Joseph's hand; and clothed him in garments of fine linen and put a gold chain around his neck. And he had him ride in the second chariot which he had; **and they cried out before him, 'Bow the knee!'** *So he set him over all the land of Egypt. Pharaoh also said to Joseph, 'I am Pharaoh, and without your consent no man may lift his hand or foot in the land of Egypt.' And Pharaoh called Joseph's name Zaphnath Paaneah.* **And he gave him a wife,** *Asenath, the daughter*

of Potiphera priest of On. So Joseph went out over all the land of
Egypt. Joseph was thirty years old..."
—**Genesis 41:25-46**

Oh, the incredible wisdom and wonderful ways of God! Remember when I told you that Joseph was homesick and wanted to go home, and that God needed him to be in prison? Well guess what? Joseph does not want to go home anymore. The incredible rise to power and miraculous prospering of Joseph is obvious. Countless sermons have focused upon this issue so I feel no need to touch on this point, but God still needs him in Egypt. To keep him there, God has given him a position that no man can turn down, a new identity (name), and a wife (family). Why go through all of this trouble to keep one man in Egypt?

Joseph is now in a position below Pharaoh in name only. All power and authority has been given to him. When Joseph passes by, the people bow the knee to him. Does this sound familiar? It should, because Joseph is the savior of his family and the savior of the gentile nation of Egypt. He is a type of Christ, a foreshadowing of the Messiah. Remarkably, Joseph was the same age at his rise to power as Jesus was when He *"...returned to Galilee in the power of the Spirit,"* (Luke 4:14) to begin His earthly ministry. They were both thirty years old. Joseph was also believed to be dead by his family and later, in a figurative sense, "brought back to life" in order to save them.

In addition, Joseph was given a gentile wife to begin a family with, just as the body of Christ consists of the congregation of gentile believers. Joseph was equal to Pharaoh in all matters with the one exception being the throne, just as Jesus is equal to God in all matters except the seating on the throne. Everyone in Joseph's presence bowed their knee, just as *"every knee shall bow and every tongue confess that Jesus Christ is Lord."* (Philippians 2:10-11)

Necessary Roughness

I would like to interject a point of critical relevance here. You may be wondering if all the episodes in Joseph's life were actually necessary.

Couldn't God have exalted Joseph to power without all the tribulation? I must impart to you emphatically that everything Joseph experienced *was absolutely* necessary. It caused Joseph to depend on God alone. It forced him to remain loyal to God culture. Joseph needed to be stripped of himself in order execute God's plan. The boy who was sold to Potiphar in Egypt was not the man God redeemed from prison. He had grown and matured through the fire of tribulation. It had to be the "High way" or no way at all—and so it was for Jesus as well.

The night before Jesus' crucifixion He prayed, *"...Oh My Father, if it is possible, let this cup pass from Me; nevertheless,* **not as I will,** *but as You will."* (Matthew 26:39) In the natural realm, Jesus did not want to go to the cross, but He knew that because it was God's way, it was the only way. That is why He answered His own question. The cross was God's way for Jesus, and prison was God's way for Joseph. God has a way for you as well. Are you willing to drink from His cup? Will you follow?

If you are new to the kingdom of God, here is a news flash: God is God and we are not. His plan is always the best, no matter what it is. In order to follow it, you must give Him all of you. He must first strip you of yourself. This will keep "Lucifer's discourse" out of you (pride; remember the "I will's"). Once you allow yourself to be broken down, and this can take quite some time and requires immense honesty with oneself, *He* will then fill in your gaps...with Himself. Only then can you walk in His power. Only then can you become a true part of God culture and fulfill the plan He has for you. That is the "now" plan. You are just beginning to see. You are catching a glimpse of "forever."

Life Preserver

"When Jacob saw there was grain in Egypt, Jacob said to his sons, 'Why do you look at one another?' And he said, 'Indeed I have heard there is grain in Egypt; go down to that place and buy for us there, that we may live and not die.'"

—Genesis 42:1-2

Right here is the reason God needed Joseph to remain in Egypt. Famine! God had the foresight and knowledge of the impending famine that would jeopardize the lives of everyone living in the Middle East at that time. Had Joseph not been imprisoned, he eventually would have made his way back home. Had that occurred, he and his entire family would have perished in the famine.

As it turns out, and this is certainly no coincidence, Joseph is in charge of the food distribution for the entire region. This once again is a Messianic parallel as Jesus proclaimed to be the bread of life, in which He likened Himself to the lifesaving Manna God sent to Israel in the Egyptian wilderness. (Exodus 16)

Joseph is later reunited with his family, and it is here that he finally understands the reason for the preceding twelve years or so of his life. He says to his brothers who are afraid he may exact revenge against them, *"But now, do not therefore be grieved or angry with yourselves because you sold me here; for **God sent me before you to preserve life**."* (Genesis 45:4-5)

Now Joseph gets it! The light bulb of revelation has lit up. Perhaps even his brothers can now see it. Remember when I stated, "Life can only be understood when looking backward?" This is the perfect example. Although Joseph was able to see and commune with God throughout his entire ordeal, it is only now that he can see the big picture. And yet, he still cannot see it all. We all see only in part. The above Scripture does not say to "preserve *your* life," it says to "preserve life." What could this possibly mean? Stay with me here, as you are nearing a revelation of God's immense power and authority.

The Big Picture

Jacob and his children now come down to Egypt and settle in the land of Goshen. There, the nation of Israel grows from a father and twelve sons to over 500,000 strong. Without Joseph's rise to power, Jacob and his twelve sons, who later became the nation of Israel, would have perished. There would have been no 500,000. That was God's *"now"* plan.

You may be thinking: "What do you mean that was the 'now' plan? It sounds like the big picture to me." God is so much bigger than you can imagine. This is simply the first page. I am now about to reveal to you how God sees and plans everything with the entire book in mind.

Let's back up for a second. Why did God call Abraham, Joseph's great grandfather, out of the land of Ur? He called him so He could make a covenant with him with a specific purpose in mind. What was that purpose? It was to make and fulfill a promise. Knowing that sin had separated man from Him, God desired to find a man through which He could bring the Messiah, the Savior of the world. So what does this have to do with Joseph? Joseph's trials were all about fulfilling the promise God made to Abraham.

Let's suppose that God had never sent Joseph to Egypt. So Joseph and his eleven brothers are "kickin' it" in the land of Canaan when the famine hits. Now they hear a rumor that there is food in Egypt so they head down to Pharaoh's place. Guess what? They have a "minor" problem. The Egyptians are a little prejudice against the Hebrews, and do you know what? "They ain't gettin' no food!" So Joseph and his family eventually perish.

The other scenario, which is perhaps even more likely, is that there would have been no food in Egypt at all. If you can recall, without Joseph, Pharaoh had no one to interpret his dreams and therefore would not have had the foresight to stockpile grain. Once again, the result is the death of the family of Israel.

Yeah…so…what's the big deal? Lots of families died in the famine. Well, yeah, that's true, but the big deal is this: of Joseph's eleven brothers, there was one named Judah. According to God, the Messiah was required to come through his lineage. That is why you have heard Jesus referred to as "the Lion of the tribe of Judah."

So if Joseph was not sent to Egypt and the family had perished in the famine, Judah would have perished with them. This means that the Messiah, Jesus Christ, would not have been born, which also means He could not die for your sin nor be raised from the dead. Thus the miracle of salvation would have been nullified and the world would have perished in its sin. You and I would not have the ability to be forgiven of sin, and entrance into heaven would be prohibited because there is no sin in heaven.

Because God "preserved life" by putting Joseph in prison, that is not the case. The Messiah *was* born, *did* die, *is* alive, and your sin *can* be forgiven. If you choose, you may reside in heaven—and *that* is God's "forever" plan.

Joseph being sent to Egypt was about the salvation of God's most valued creation, **you!** *"For God so loved the world that He gave His only begotten Son. That whosoever may believe in Him shall not perish, but have everlasting life."* (John 3:16) God culture is always about the salvation of God's beloved people. Billions will live "forever" in heaven as a result of Joseph's imprisonment.

Now, do you want to hear something really amazing? This really hammers home God's "forever" plan and His amazing love for each and every one of us: when God sent Joseph to Egypt, approximately four thousand years ago, He was not only thinking about Joseph and his eleven brothers. He was not even thinking only about Jesus Christ. **He was thinking about you!** Foresight's 20/20.

— CHAPTER 3 —

Tribulation and Persecution

I have often wondered how I would react if confronted with a life and death decision. I am not one hundred percent sure whether I have ever consciously faced one. Have you? I have this fantasy that I would be some sort of evangelical superman, as if it would be like being in a bar fight in my younger days, but the truth is that no one could ever know how he or she will react until you are actually faced with the choice and forced to confront your greatest fear.

Would I stand up and be martyred like the prophets of old, or would I shrink back, hide, and deny Jesus just like St. Peter did when faced with the crucifixion of Jesus Christ? I have been in perilous situations before, but the type of persecution I am referring to goes beyond potential danger. The outcome of this decision is absolute and final.

In America and most parts of the Western world, life and death decisions most likely arise in the form of swerving one way or the other when operating an automobile, or even more likely, deciding what treatment to pursue when faced with a life-threatening illness. I am not trying to trivialize any of this. It is serious stuff, but it is not persecution—and it is not by choice. You may also encounter a number of indirect lifestyle choices that ultimately result in your living or dying, such as deciding whether or not to implement an exercise program along with the proper diet. I think you get the gist of what I am saying. Religious peril in the West is rare. It is simply not a part of Western culture.

Most of us will never have to make such a choice. More often than not, if we do, we have probably become the victim of a violent crime. Even a drug addict shooting up is not consciously deciding to die, even if the ensuing overdose proves fatal. Can you even imagine facing death over your religion? For most people in the world today, the very concept of dying for one's religion is unfathomable. Particularly in the West, we believe religious persecution was for yesteryear. Martyrdom is an inconceivable thought in the West. This is not the case everywhere in the world today

In many parts of the third world, such as the Far East, Middle East and Africa, your religion may be the determining factor in matters such as success or failure and, yes, even life and death. In Indonesia, a country that I am very familiar with, your religion is indicated right on your identification card. This, which is denoted for everyone to see, oftentimes determines whether or not you get the job you applied for, the house you bid on, and even the favor of your own family and friends. In most parts of the world, persecution remains alive and well… and thankfully, so does the Lord.

It is in places like these that we still witness the miraculous. I have seen it firsthand. I personally met a man from Indonesia who had a scar encircling nearly the entire circumference of his neck. In May of 1998, in the capital city of Jakarta, he was thrown into a mass grave with his head all but hacked off during the riots resulting from the Asian financial crisis, which gave rise to a tremendous bout of persecution in that nation. His only crime was being Christian in a Muslim nation. Do you know where his attackers found him? He was studying to be a pastor and the seminary was the first place invaded. His aggressors were well aware of the opportunity and he was well aware of the risk.

When I asked him if he was bitter, he looked at me kind of funny. His scar is a badge of courage. He is a living testimony and, to those who believe, he is an actual miracle. I have seen the photographs. This man was all but dead, and yet he lives. I am not sure how his external jugular vein remained intact. He told me that he felt God reconstruct his neck vertebrae. He felt the actual cracking, popping and fusing together as he lay in the grave and, subsequently, the hospital bed. Somehow he wasn't ensanguined, that is, dead from blood loss. He was given a second chance.

In what most would consider an evil and vicious attack, this gentle young man has recognized an opportunity that very few have had the privilege to engage in. He believes, as I do, that God did not just allow the attack, He purposed it. In fact, he found his purpose in it, and he gained entry into the company of quite a few unique and historically famous individuals. You might even know some of them yourself.

This unique culture includes individuals such as the Apostle Paul, St. Peter, Stephen the Martyr, and even Jesus Christ of Nazareth. All were persecuted and even killed for the sake of spreading the good news of the Gospel, which is for the salvation of all of mankind. Just like the amazing individuals you are about to read about, he has found the key that gained him entry into the kingdom of God—tribulation and persecution. Check out this excerpt from the Book of Acts. It is quite similar in nature to what happened to my friend.

> "Then Jews from Antioch and Iconium came there; and having persuaded the multitudes, they stoned Paul and dragged him out of the city, **supposing him dead.** However, when the disciples gathered around him, he rose up and went into the city. And the next day he departed with Barnabas to Derbe. And when they had preached the gospel to that city and made many disciples, they returned to Lystra, Iconium, and Antioch, strengthening the souls of the disciples, exhorting them to continue in the faith, and saying, 'we **must through many tribulations enter the kingdom of God."**
> —**Acts 14:19-22**

It's Not About You

As a result of meeting such amazing individuals who have completely discounted their own lives for the sake of Jesus Christ, I have come to a realization that has set me completely free. I have written this chapter so you can experience the same liberty. It is so amazingly simple and yet at the same time so immensely difficult to apprehend. Once you do, you will never experience life in the same manner. You will encounter a paradigm shift in your view of both God and man. You will become a part of God culture. The epiphany that I am describing to you is simply this: it's not about me.

Once I got right with God, that is, once I repented my old ways and accepted Jesus Christ as my Lord and Savior, life and the trials associated with being alive became no longer just about me. Look at all of the tribulation Joseph, whom we read about in the last chapter, encountered in his life and not one iota of it was about him. It was all about God's greater plan for him and his brothers, the line of the Messiah, and ultimately you and me.

When I come to terms with the fact that God is using me for something greater, no matter what I am going through, the problems no longer matter. It's not about me. They are still difficult. I do not enjoy them, but I can lay aside all of the guilt, condemnation and especially worry. I can sit back, relax, get down on my knees and pray to the Almighty Creator of the Universe for wisdom and understanding, confidently knowing that He will pull me through the situation, no matter what it looks like or how it feels, because it's not about me. It is about God and His purpose for using me.

With that in mind, here is the first and foremost concept to understand when attempting to discern how and why God is using us. The key to discovering God's purpose for your life and entering God culture is coming to the realization that **God never calls and anoints you only for you.** Your gifts and your talents are for the benefit of those around you. You will benefit and you will experience the power of God, but God never wants you to keep what He gives you to yourself.

Just like He did with Joseph, He needs to shake up our lives from time to time in order to push us forward in His kingdom. Just as God is a giver and a sharer of **all** that He has, *"For God so loved the world **that He gave His only begotten Son,"*** (John 3:16), He is encouraging you to do the same. In fact, He is transforming you to *be* the same. Do you understand the difference? God is not calling you to *do* something for Him. He is calling you to *become one* with Him. God gave you His all. He gave you Himself, and He continues to do this day in and day out, even when we rebel against Him. Are you willing to do the same for Him? Overcoming tribulation and persecution is how you prove it.

Jesus Christ is our ultimate example. His chief purpose for being born was to die for the purpose of fulfilling the Word of God. His suffering allows you to become one with God in eternity. Eternal life was garnered by His experiencing temptation, tribulation, persecution, and ultimately martyrdom—all things that we Christians may ourselves face one day.

Will you experience martyrdom? Only God knows. Oftentimes we encounter situations, both voluntary and involuntary, that can place us in harm's way. This may result from something as simple as traveling to a foreign country. For example, take John and Wanda Casias of Amarillo, Texas, who were martyred in the mission field in Mexico in service of the Lord. I recently read of their plight, and according to their former church's Assistant Pastor Jeff York, "They knew it was getting dangerous in Mexico, and yet they decided to stay," he said. "They made that decision."

Both were found dead with electrical cords wrapped around their necks. It is not known whether it was a break-in or if they had fallen prey to the drug cartels that objected to their presence. What *is* known is that they changed the lives of countless villagers while they were ministering there and, as a result, many will reside in eternity with them. They knew the potential danger, and yet they decided to accept the consequences of serving the Lord and stayed. In knowing what I know spiritually, I have to believe that they never considered this life to be their ultimate destination. If you believe in Jesus Christ, it is not yours either.

"Therefore we are always confident, knowing that when we are absent from the body, we are present with the Lord." (2 Corinthians 5:6) Their confidence was sustained in knowing that they belonged to Jesus Christ, and that nothing—not tribulation, persecution, distress, famine, nakedness, or even death—could separate them from His love (Romans 8:35). *"Yet in all these things we are more than conquerors through Him who loved us."* (Romans 8:37)

In the end, we will all experience death. Our hope lies in the One who has overcome death. That is our culture. John and Wanda Casias longed for a better place. Through the power of Christ, they have conquered the grave. They are one with God.

We may never know the earthly purpose for their death, but God does. Perhaps an entire village in Mexico will one day know as well. One of my all-time favorite movies is *The Last Samurai*. In it, Tom Cruise and the character of Katsumoto, the leader of the Samurai warriors, engage in several conversations regarding Katsumoto's search for the perfect cherry blossom as well as the concept of dying a "good death." A good death is one that is honorable and brave while fighting for what one believes in.

During the final battle in the movie as they are struggling to retain the Samurai culture, Katsumoto is struck down by the American's brand new technology, the Gatling gun. As he lay in Tom Cruise's arms awaiting his final breath, he gazes across the battlefield and sees a vision. Off in the distance is a group of Japanese cherry trees in full bloom. As he begins his slide into eternity, he peers into Tom Cruise's eyes and exclaims, "They're all perfect," and breathes his last breath in this life.

I can't help but believe that John and Wanda had a similar experience while breathing their last breaths as well. What I find interesting is the Japanese cherry tree, often referred to as "Sakura" in the Japanese culture, is known as being a lasting metaphor regarding the ephemeral (or short-lived) nature of life. Although no one likes to think in these terms, the ephemeral nature of life is often the call for those engaging in God culture. Physical death is every man's final destination. There is no need to fear this. Death is not the end, for those of us who believe it is merely our new, or secondary birth. It is a new beginning. In Christ, life springs eternal.

"For this corruptible must put on incorruption, and this mortal must put on immortality. So when this corruptible has put on incorruption, and this mortal has put on immortality, then shall be brought to pass the saying that is written: 'Death is swallowed up in victory. O Death, where is your sting?'"
—1 Corinthians 15:53-55

With the exception of Jesus Christ, no man ever embarks on a journey with death as their ultimate goal, even when the risk of peril is well known. In God culture, however, death is often times God's highest call. It was for Jesus, and it was for John and Wanda Casias, but in their case the metaphors were switched. The perfect cherry blossom was Jesus Christ, who gazed into *John and Wanda's* eyes and proclaimed, "They're perfect." It was a good death.

By placing the eternal interest of an entire village above even their own lives, John and Wanda achieved the highest level of God culture. Jesus stated it this way, *"Greater love has no one than this, than to lay down one's life for his friends."* (John 15:13) I would be honored to one day hear those same words from our Lord. They were perfect.

John and Wanda will receive their just reward in heaven. Although they did not know the time and place of their ultimate end, Jesus knew from day one what would happen to Him, and yet He remained willing. Was Jesus a martyr? As Sarah Palin would say, "You betcha." He died for God's purpose, which is the salvation of your soul, as well as, for the countless billions who have and will accept God's sacrifice.

Keep in mind that Jesus' death and resurrection was not about Him. He was already perfect and one with the Father. Jesus' death was about the whole of humanity. As we learned in the previous chapter, that is how God operates. That's His culture. *That is* God culture. He is always about the bigger picture, and it is through faith that we must accept it.

Like Jesus, when you begin to experience tribulation and persecution, God's ultimate purpose is not only about you. You are simply a tool, a highly prized and beloved instrument of righteousness, but, nonetheless, a tool.

We read earlier in Acts 14:22, *"...we must through many tribulations enter the kingdom of God...."* I could also state it this way: "We must through many tribulations enter God culture." Tribulation has always been God's way. Do you hear this being taught in church today? This was a major doctrinal issue within the early church.

Many of us today feel as Bill Maher does, the host of the television show, "Politically Incorrect," who stated, "Let's face it: God has a big ego problem. Why do we always have to worship Him?" The truth is that we must do things God's way, and persecution was confirmation of being in God's will. It was proof that you were preaching the true Gospel, that you were part of God culture. Where has that gone?

> *"Man is a messenger who forgot the message."*
> **—Abraham Joshua Heschel**

The Kingdom of God

The phrase "enter the kingdom of God" as used in Acts 14:22, is not referring to going to heaven. It is a reference to entering the realm of the Spirit, or more plainly stated, it is entering into God's way of doing things. This is the very definition of God culture, being willing to conduct your life according to what God deems to be right and *not* what society *thinks* is right.

To take this even further, if you have never experienced tribulation and/or persecution, you have not truly entered the realm of the Spirit. That is, if you have never suffered while being innocent, you have probably not begun to do things God's way. Persecution is a test of your righteousness. If you have or are being persecuted, it is time to determine what God is doing. He is trying to reach someone—either you or someone around you.

A kingdom, or realm, refers to a government. In this instance, we are referring to entering the "government" or "kingdom" of God. The word "government" actually means the form or system of rule by which a community or state is governed. To "govern" means to make and administer the public policy and affairs of and to exercise sovereign authority in. Finally, to "rule" actually means a principle or regulation governing conduct, action and procedure.

In this instance, to enter "the kingdom of God," which means to execute the actual procedure of doing things in God's way, means we must by definition experience, and in some cases suffer, tribulation and persecution. According to Acts 14:22, experiencing tribulation and persecution is God culture. It is the way He does things.

Please do not be discouraged by this. God's goal is not to punish you. It is to establish you. The sad reality is that whenever and wherever Christians become too comfortable, the light of Christ begins to dim. Luxury seems to be the death of God culture. People enter their comfort zones and it becomes next to impossible to move them out of it, except by means of an event or events whether fortunate or unfortunate. Unfortunate seems to work best.

People respond differently to various situations where they cannot quite predict the outcome. More often than not, this requires pain. If you are experiencing this, do not be afraid. Get closer to God. Do not run from Him; run to Him. The Holy Spirit is more than sufficient to supply you with enough power and courage to overcome any situation that life can throw at you—even death.

A Righteous Judge

The economic crisis of 2008 is a perfect example of pain. As the economy crumbled and folks lost their livelihoods, their futures became quite uncertain. It is oftentimes such as these that we fall to our knees and cry out to God for help.

America became very "religious" on September *12,* 2001. Why? Because we were severely persecuted on September *11,* 2001. The unfortunate events of 9/11 caused us discomfort, pain, fear, and for about 3,000 Americans, it cost them the ultimate price—their lives. We were instantly removed from our comfort zone.

Did God cause, or at the very least allow, the attack of America on 9/11? I will let you be the judge of that, but it would not be the first time God judged a nation. God judged Sodom and Gomorrah; He judged

Nineveh; and I believe in a small way He may have judged America as we had become very comfortable and had for quite some time begun to move away from the ways of Almighty God.

I do not believe, however, that He was judging the individuals who perished. We will all stand before Him some day and then we will be judged. Unfortunately when God judges a nation or city, people oftentimes get in the way. We do not always know why people die but our righteous Judge has His reasons for everything. I would simply ask that you consider His mercy in this matter as our nation still stands. The same cannot be said for countless others throughout history.

Brave New World

Look at the founding of America, for example. It is a fact, no, it is an actual truth that the American government was formed with its primary base being the Word of God—the Holy Bible, to be more specific. All you need to do is read the Constitution of the United States to figure this out or say the Pledge of Allegiance. You know, "…one nation, under God.…" I know, many of you will argue, "…but that was added in the 1950s." You're missing the point. We are a nation of believers in God.

As a matter of fact, if you are not motivated enough to actually read the Constitution, just take a trip to Washington D.C. and visit the monuments there. It will not take very long for you to figure out that our forefathers were believers in God too. From the very beginning of our nation, God was part of our culture.

The reason the Pilgrims even got on a boat and sailed to this wonderful "land of promise" was to be able to worship Jesus Christ in Spirit and in truth without the interference of the English government, which required them to worship according to the state-run Church of England. They were being persecuted in England for their beliefs so they got on a couple of boats and left. Amazingly, the United States of America was the result.

The Chinese suffer similar persecution to this very day. In the 1970s and 80s, it looked like the Book of Acts in China. The result has been a massive outpouring of the Holy Spirit and a rapidly growing underground church chock full of brand new believers.

Here we are, two hundred thirty plus years later with countless Americans having spilled their blood for our freedom, and we are allowing the rapidly becoming anti-Christ American government to dictate how and where we worship the Lord, if we even have the desire to do so. If that sounds over the top, try having your children pray in school. Try hanging the Ten Commandments in schools or any public building for that matter. Our life in Christ is not supposed to be compartmentalized. It is meant to be on display.

> *"And these words which I command you today shall be in your heart. You shall teach them diligently to your children, and you shall talk of them when you sit in your house, when you walk by the way, when you lie down, and when you rise up. You shall bind them as a sign on your hand, and they shall be as frontlets between your eyes. You shall write them on the doorposts of your house and on your gates."*
> **—Deuteronomy 6:6-9**

Try declaring the name of Jesus, the basis for early American political thought, in our public schools. Try it in Congress. You can now be sworn into office using the Q'ran. You will learn very quickly that Christianity continues to suffer tribulation and persecution. You will also learn very quickly that American culture is not God culture.

I have recently learned that Halloween is America's fastest growing holiday in terms of monies spent in celebration. Halloween is not just some fun little harmless fantasy day. It is a celebration of witchcraft, demonism, ghosts, ghouls, fear and death—all of which God abhors. If you don't believe that, just take a look at the decorations on your neighbor's lawn, or perhaps even your own.

More dollars are being spent by "Christians" on Halloween than any other holiday in America, with the exception of Christmas. It is bigger than Easter, the day we celebrate the resurrection of the Lord, and it is quickly catching up to Christmas, which by the way is no longer about the birth of Christ either. It is more about the end-of-the-year sales numbers for the corporate stockholder than it is about God's obliteration of sin.

I am going to ask you a question and I want you to be honest: What do you and your children primarily look forward to on Christmas, especially if you have young children? Is it the celebration of the birth of the Lord? Or is it opening presents and waiting for Santa Claus? I would venture to guess that your kids are more in love with Santa than Jesus Christ. I am sure, for most of you, that your children know and talk more about Santa.

Children actually believe they can receive more from a fictional Santa Claus than they can from the one and only living God who created them and the entire universe. Are you okay with that? It would be my guess that if you were to attempt to eliminate Santa, or even the Christmas tree, from your holiday celebration, you would be persecuted by your friends, co-workers and even your family. I know because I have done it. Trust me, it did not go well—even in my own house.

America's lamp is dimming. Our culture is changing. Many of our "Christians" are Christian in name only. They may even go to church, but that is where it ends for many of us. Do you want to hear some proof of that? A survey was done asking American Christians to quote their favorite Bible verse. Something like seventy percent of those surveyed quoted, "The Lord helps those who help themselves." Sounds good, right? There is only one problem. That "Scripture" does not appear in the Bible. In fact, it's not even true. God primarily helps those who *can't* help themselves. *"My grace is sufficient for you, for My strength is made perfect in weakness."* (2 Corinthians 12:9) That is the purpose of persecution. It connects you to God.

You and your children do not need Santa—you need Jesus. You need the Word of God. Trust me, when you tell them the truth of who truly matters, they will not be disappointed. Try spending Christmas with Jesus this year. Forget about Santa. Open up a Bible, read the Christmas story, read the crucifixion story, and tell them of the best gift they can possibly have, which is Christ given to us. Teach them of God's great love and mercy. Keep God culture alive. Then open your presents. Make it an act of worship, celebration and thanksgiving of who God is and what God has given you.

While you are at it, refrain from participating in Halloween.

"...I do not want you to have fellowship with demons. You cannot drink the cup of the Lord and the cup of demons; you cannot partake of the Lord's Table and of the table of demons. Or do we provoke the Lord to jealousy? Are we stronger than He?"

—1 Corinthians 10:20-22

If your kids want candy, buy them some. My wife and I committed to this some time ago and our kids do not miss it. As a matter of fact, now that we have spent the time teaching them why we do not celebrate Halloween, they think it is a stupid holiday. Why would you spend three hundred sixty-four and one quarter days worshipping God and then one day per year worshipping hell (it has actually become about a month now, thanks to capitalism)... and you have to worry about some psychopath poisoning your candy. It is a twisted thought process.

No Pain No Gain

I will warn you: Satan does not like us intruding on his day. You will be persecuted for it and so will your children. I have had numerous parents become quite angry with me when asked to state my position. Your children will experience tremendous pressure when everyone around them is talking about their Halloween costumes and then one asks them, "What are you going to be for Halloween?" You must prepare them. They must have an answer. You must teach them the Word of God.

Give them understanding and the pressure and persecution they experience will actually be good for them. It will teach them to stand up for what they believe in. It will teach them to stand up for Christ. God continually warns us to, *"...give no place to the devil."* (Ephesians 4:27) If He warns us, we would be well-served to heed His advice. We are not stronger than God and we cannot partake of the Lord's Table and the table of demons. I have tried and it does not work.

Everything you need to know about God is contained within His Word. It has been meticulously preserved and harmoniously arranged for the purpose of our getting to know the ways and personality of the God we serve. It is a memoir of His culture and, therefore, I encourage you to become familiar with it and with Him.

A large part of being a Christian is to have an understanding and a familiarity with the Word of God. This allows us to skillfully apply it to our lives while, at the same time, grow to love the Lord by developing an intimate relationship with Him. This requires a certain amount of diligence and dedication. Some may even say pain. In time you will become more comfortable with His principles, concepts and culture. Being born into a Christian home and ignoring the Word of God qualifies you as an agnostic at best. Philippians 2:12 says we must, *"...work out our own salvation with fear and trembling."*

I want to warn you: you cannot pick and choose what goes in and what comes out of the Word of Truth. That is God's job and it is only truth when preserved and contained as a whole. God and His Word are one. *"In the beginning was the Word, and the Word was with God, and **the Word was God**... And **the Word became flesh** and dwelt among us."* (John 1:1 and 14)

This is why I always capitalize the "W" when referring to God's Word. The Spirit of the Word is also the Spirit of God. Your relationship with God must be developed through and based on the Word of God and the Lord Jesus Christ. He cannot be left out. When He is, we begin to experience such doctrines as, "All religions are the same," or "All religions will make you a good person," or one that I recently heard when having a conversation with a gentleman on the golf course, "It doesn't matter to me what religion you are. I'm just happy you have one."

It is my opinion that these doctrines are a result of the fight or flight response when experiencing persecution. Who wants to be labeled a Jesus freak or some kind of religious weirdo? It is easier to just avoid the issue and blend in. Unfortunately, as a result of diluting our faith in an effort to fit in, eventually our culture becomes oblivious to persecution's purpose and God is eliminated from society. Sound familiar? Persecution does not have to maim or kill a man to be effective. It simply needs to alienate one from the truth. *"There is a way that seems right to a man, but the end is the way of death."* (Proverbs 14:12)

The conditioning of a society is similar to boiling a frog. Scientists have discovered that if you put a frog in a pot of water and introduce heat, the frog does not realize the water temperature is rising. It slowly acclimates to the new temperature until it gets so hot that the frog dies without ever attempting to escape from the pot.

We see this same phenomenon occur when introducing changes into world cultures. For example, Hitler wasn't exterminating the Jews from day one. He conditioned Germany with a series of small steps that continually built upon one another. Then without even realizing what was happening, the Germans found that they were in the middle of the holocaust—just as America is guilty of its own holocaust today. According to the **Centers for Disease Control** and Prevention, nearly fifty million legal abortions, and still counting, having been performed in the United States since 1973, and those are conservative estimates with the political system as its protector.

We have been conditioned to believe a baby is not even alive until it reaches a certain number of months in the womb. Some would even argue up to the point of birth. The majority of teenage boys would opt for abortion as option number one without ever considering the life of the baby they just fathered. Sadly, their female counter parts have been conditioned to agree. They have been boiled like frogs.

This discussion is not intended to condemn anyone, but rather to reveal the truth of what persecution looks like in the West. The deception of the aforementioned doctrines and many others like them has become so immensely dangerous because there is no basis for truth in them. Life begins at conception. All religions are not the same and there is absolute truth.

When a society becomes apathetic toward the truth with no understanding of God's Word, it loses its spiritual reference point. As a result, we have begun to experience moral decay, a spiritual vacuum, and a day-by-day desensitizing of the human condition. Simply watching television is a daily reminder of this sad truth.

So what does society do? They persecute those who stand for the truth and replace God with humanism or any other lie that blinds them to their true condition. Unfortunately, as we merely sit back in our easy chairs and watch, we continually see God's children die in their sins with no Savior. Why does this happen? because we are afraid of a little discomfort. No pain no gain.

Find Strength in Your Weakness

This is not the case in many countries where life is not so pleasant and full of luxury. The nations that are experiencing the greatest Christian revival are those where persecution seems to be the greatest. China and Indonesia are two prime examples that come to mind. To be a Christian in China means to risk beatings, tortures, humiliations, imprisonment, and even death.

Several years ago, three schoolgirls were brutally attacked in Indonesia while walking home from school. Two were beheaded with machetes and one was savagely injured. Why? because they believed Jesus is Lord. Yet, in the midst of all this danger and persecution, the Lord Jesus reigns. Day after day we see a multitude of miracles, the greatest of these being the hundreds and even thousands of previously Muslim, Buddhist, Hindu, and even atheistic people entered into the Lamb's Book of Life. God is most powerful where human weakness abounds.

In America and countless other Western societies, we sit in our comfortable living rooms with our three televisions, two computers, two or more cars, three or more types of video games, big fat bank accounts, and our prosperity doctrine with rooms full of as many Bibles as we can pay for, yet they remain unread. Some are not even opened and, even worse, are not acted upon. Hey, I'm not bashing prosperity. In fact, I'm all for it, but with what end in sight? Is it to get rich or is it to glorify the kingdom?

"Blessed is he who considers the poor; the Lord will deliver him out of trouble, the Lord will preserve him and keep him alive, and he will be blessed on the earth."

—Psalm 41:1-3

I recently read that an entire underground church in China existed on a single torn page of the Bible containing merely one paragraph of scripture. They were unable to obtain even one Bible, and yet their church prospered. Money glorifies God when it is not merely used as a tool for selfish personal gain, but rather as an entrance into the "kingdom of God." No wonder the Lord is shaking up the world's economies! He is implementing God culture.

The average American believes, "God helps those who help themselves." As stated earlier, God helps those who *can't* help themselves. That's where His strength lies, and that is where our opportunities lie.

"...God has chosen the foolish things of the world to confound the wise, and God has chosen the weak things of the world to confound the mighty...."
—1 Corinthians 1:27

It is in your most trying times, when no one else can help, that you turn to God. What we must learn to understand is that for God, it is all about connecting with you. His only desire is for you to know and love Him. It is in your weakness that He is able to gain your attention and give you strength. This is when He can consume you. This is when you allow Him to use you, His body, to help accomplish His will. To enter the "kingdom of God" and ultimately our eternal Kingdom where Jesus alone presides requires a little—and sometimes a great deal—of discomfort.

Preparing For the Mission
When studying the Word of God, there is one book that illustrates the spread of the gospel like no other. That is the Book of the Acts of the Apostles. In the Gospel records, we see Jesus making disciples. We get to know our Savior. We learn of His unfailing love and mercy, and we experience the work of the cross. It is oh so glorious! If the Bible ended right there, it would be enough, but it does not end there.

When we enter into the Book of Acts, we discover the outpouring of the Holy Spirit. We see ordinary human beings become full of the power of God. Weakness turns to boldness. Fear turns to courage, and we see the disciples transformed into apostles before our very eyes.

A "disciple" is a person who is a pupil or an adherent to the doctrines of another. A disciple begins as a pupil and later becomes a follower of that person. "Disciple" is the root of our English word "discipline." To be a disciple of Christ means you are proficient with living according to the ways, or disciplines, of Christ. In essence, you have prepared and "disciplined" yourself to adhere to Jesus' lifestyle. It has become your culture. This is why it is impossible to truly be a Christian without knowledge of the Word of God.

An "apostle," on the other hand, is the title of a person or persons sent on a mission. In the Book of Acts, we find these apostles being sent on missions all over Asia, Europe, and the Middle East. The million dollar question is: who sent them? Furthermore, how and why were they sent? To answer these two questions, let's delve into Scripture.

So You Want to Be Like Jesus?

We pick up where Stephen the Apostle has received great courage from the Holy Spirit and is delivering a bone chilling message to Israel: *"You stiff necked and uncircumcised in heart and ears! Which of the prophets did your father's not persecute? And they killed those who foretold the coming of the Just One, of whom you now have become the betrayers and murderers, who have received the law by the direction of angels and have not kept it.'"* (Acts 7:51-53)

First of all, allow me to reiterate something of vital importance. God's way has always been for those who truly speak His Word to be persecuted. We see it all over the Old Testament. Jeremiah was persecuted. Isaiah was persecuted. Joseph, David, Samson… all the way through to John the Baptist who had his head removed by Herod—they all suffered persecution. They all foreshadowed the Suffering Servant, Jesus Christ.

I cannot tell you how many people I have heard exclaim, "I want to be like Jesus." Are you sure you want to make that claim? Are you willing to commit to that? Yes, when it is fun and glorious. We all want the ability to heal, prophesy, raise the dead, and preach heart-wrenching sermons, but how about the ability to suffer? It is as much a part of Christian culture as prosperity, healing, prophesying, and preaching. Do you really want to be like Jesus, the *Suffering* Servant? Remember, you must take the good with the bad.

I love Job's response to his wife after she declared that Job in his illness should curse God and die. He stated, *"You speak as one of the foolish women speaks. Shall we indeed accept good from God, and shall we not accept adversity?"* (Job 2:10) Tribulation and persecution is undoubtedly a major aspect of the Christian life and culture. To think otherwise is foolish. What most do not realize is that Job's response to his wife was not in regard to his illness. It was in regard to the tribulation and persecution he had been experiencing in the previous months. God does not make or even want you to be sick, but He will use tribulation and persecution to mold your character into His very own image.

We must realize this is normal in God culture and see through the trouble. As you will soon discover, *it's all good,* even the adversity. With God, there is no bad. There is just purpose. When you have an understanding of the "forever," you gain God's vision and will soon experience joy even in, and sometimes as a result of, your temporal suffering.

Back to Stephen: *"When they heard these things they were cut to the heart, and they gnashed at him with their teeth."* (Acts 7:54)

The truth of God will *always* cut right to the heart of the sinner. Believe me, Satan does not appreciate the truth and he *will* lash out at you. A careful study of the Book of Job reveals that this is what was happening in his life. Satan was lashing out at Job. The spirit of anti-Christ was also lashing out at Stephen. Just imagine how angry and convicted one must feel to actually gnash their teeth at a person. I get a picture of them acting like rabid dogs, showing and gritting their teeth while salivating at their potential prey.

Also, take note of the boldness with which Stephen spoke. This can only be done under the direction of the Holy Spirit. If you attempt this outside of the Spirit, you will cause more harm than good. There comes a time and an anointing by which your potential convert may need a good tongue-lashing. Please allow it to be God's tongue doing the lashing, and not your own.

Make Love Not War

> *"But he, being full of the Holy Spirit, gazed into heaven and saw the glory of God, and Jesus standing at the right hand of God, and said, 'Look! I see the heavens opened and the Son of Man* **standing** *at the right hand of God!'*
>
> *"Then they cried out with a loud voice, stopped their ears, and ran at him with one accord; and they cast him out of the city and stoned him. And the witnesses laid down their clothes at the feet of a young man named Saul. And they stoned Stephen as he was calling on God and saying, 'Lord Jesus, receive my spirit.' Then he knelt down and cried out with a loud voice, 'Lord do not charge them with this sin.' And when he had said this, he fell asleep."*
>
> **—Acts 7:55-60**

Let me begin with the description of Jesus standing in the first passage. Normally Jesus is seated at the right hand of the Father, but in this instance we find Jesus standing. The persecution and martyrdom of Stephen caused Jesus to rise into action. So you may ask, "If Jesus rose to action, why didn't He save Stephen?" The truth is that He did. He saved Stephen at the cross, the same place He saved you. You are only perceiving what your natural eyes can see, but what do God's eyes see?

In this instance, Jesus stood and reached *down* for Stephen (remember: absent from the body, present with the Lord). He also reached *out* with a different purpose. God always has a "forever" plan, so do not forget that Saul of Tarsus, who later became the Apostle Paul, was on the scene. He witnessed the event first hand *in opposition* to the kingdom of God. As a result, he had a complete understanding of those who objected to the validity of Jesus Christ. He went on to write a great deal of the New Testament, more than half of its content. This scene was part of his ultimate destiny and prepared him for the mission to come.

Persecution always has a purpose and invariably causes Jesus to act. In this instance, the death of Stephen was ultimately about Saul, not Stephen. Think about that for a moment. It was about the *persecutor,* not the *persecuted.* I bet you have never considered that God is working on both sides of the human condition. He loves both the evil and the righteous, and so must we.

"He makes His sun rise on the evil and on the good, and sends rain on the just and on the unjust." (Matthew 5:45) God loves both sides equally. Paul's writings have influenced countless Christians and, as you read this discourse, even you and me. Ultimately, the stoning of Stephen was not about either him or Paul, it was about the salvation of all humanity.

With that in mind, I want you to take note of the behavior of a true martyr for God. We see Stephen, while being stoned, praying that God will forgive the sins of his persecutors. We witness the exact opposite in Islam today. Although George W. Bush labeled Islam to be a religion of peace, in many cases, the Q'ran does not teach peace at all. It promotes war, and it teaches imperialism. This does not mean that all Muslims are evil. I know and love quite a few Muslim people. My wife's entire family is Muslim. I have many wonderful Muslim friends and we sincerely love each other and would never consider harming one another.

Our religious difference, however, and the point that I am making, is that nowhere in the Bible did Jesus ever ask His followers to kill, persecute, lie, cheat or steal. Conversely, the Q'ran not only condones these things, a case can be made that it encourages all of the above for the sake of spreading Islam. Islam persecutes; Christianity is persecuted. These are two distinctly different doctrines. They are vastly different cultures.

Stephen, as well as every true Christian, was harmless in a physical sense. Our fight is not physical; it is spiritual. *"For we do not wrestle against flesh and blood, but against principalities, against powers, **against the rulers of the darkness of this age,** against spiritual wickedness in the heavenly places."*(Ephesians 6:12)

Even in the midst of Stephen's most gut wrenching discourse, he acted in love. He never lashed out or cursed his persecutors. He loved his enemies to the very end, even while they were bashing in his skull. In the midst of a brutal beating, we behold Stephen praying forgiveness over his aggressors. Likewise, we discover the same behavior in Jesus. *"And when they had come to the place called Calvary, there they crucified Him, and the criminals, one on the right hand and one on the left. Then Jesus said, 'Father forgive them, for they know not what they do.'"* (Luke 23:33-34)

This is the behavior required to be like Jesus. Do you still want to be like Him? Although so many of us will still answer yes, my true question is, can you be? Do you have the desire and the ability to enter that which is without a doubt the most challenging aspect of God culture? Eternal life lies on the other side. Unfortunately, when left to our own devices, history has proven the answer to be a resounding no.

This behavior does not manifest itself unless one is truly filled with the Holy Spirit. We did not hear any of the criminals offering forgiveness, and they were guilty. Forgiveness is not part of the criminal culture. It is considered to be weakness. My hero Jesus was totally and completely innocent, as was Stephen. He had committed no crime. Let me give you an example of not just the strength required, but the incredible power required to forgive.

Just imagine what happened to Jesus. Put yourself in His place for a brief moment. He endured four-inch nails pounded through His wrists exactly at the base of the nerve. Reach down and touch the top of your foot. Go ahead...do it. Now imagine those same nails being driven through the bones of your feet as the pain surges throughout your entire being. Meanwhile, shards of tree bark rip into your whip-shredded back as they drag and stretch you across a fallen tree trunk. These were not the smooth sanded crosses that you see on a crucifix.

Imagine the pain of a crown of twisted thorns being rammed into your skull. Then you are brutally battered with sticks, causing a surge of pain from your head to the base of your pelvis. We are not talking about twigs here. This felt more like being hammered with miniature Billy clubs, and the thorns pierced every nerve in the base of His skull. You have been spit on, beaten, whipped, and humiliated. You are naked and profusely bleeding. You have had your beard plucked out. You thirst, and you are weakened from blood loss. You are totally innocent. As the nails thrust through, you pray for the *forgiveness* of your brutal attackers. That requires immense power.

That is the behavior of a true Godly martyr. Not these psycho terrorists we find committing mass murder and killing innocent men, women and children regardless of religion. That is not a martyr. That is a murderer. In fact, it is cowardly. There is no power in it. The God of love does not require *yours* or anyone else's blood. *He required only His own.* That is love. That's mercy. Obtaining "forever" is the intended result of the culture of tribulation and persecution, with Jesus as our prime example.

Spread the Word

"Now Saul was consenting to his (Stephen's) *death. At the time a great persecution arose against the church which was at Jerusalem; and they were all scattered throughout the regions of Judea and Samaria, except the apostles. And devout men carried Stephen to his burial, and made great lamentation over him. As for Saul, he made havoc of the church, entering every house, and dragging off men and women, committing them to prison.*

"Therefore those who were scattered went everywhere preaching the Word. Then Philip went down to the city of Samaria and preached Christ to them. And the multitudes with one accord heeded the things spoken by Philip, hearing and seeing the miracles that he did. For unclean spirits, crying with a loud voice came out of many who were possessed; and many who were paralyzed and lame were healed. And there was great joy in that city."
—Acts 8:1-8

Did you catch that? If not, read it again. Did you see the result of the persecution? First, do not skip what may seem to be the most inconsequential word within the passage, which is the word "therefore." It is perhaps the most important word contained within this Scripture, and we normally just read right past it. As a result, we miss nearly one hundred percent of what God is attempting to communicate to us.

The word "therefore" in Acts 8:3 means "as a result of." What does "therefore" apply to in this instance? It applies to what is contained above it. If we read what is truly summarized by the word "therefore," you arrive at the following: As a result of the great persecution that arose against the church and Saul making havoc of the church by forcibly entering every house and dragging off men and women and sending them to prison, those who were scattered went everywhere preaching the Word.

What we oftentimes perceive as total disaster results in the glorification of our Father. This is what is meant by *"...all things work together for good to those who love God, to those who are called according to **His purpose**."* (Romans 8:28) Always remember: "now" vs. "forever." Forever is our culture. It is our ultimate goal and our final destination.

Second, the persecution caused God's people to be scattered and the Word to be preached where it would not have been under more peaceful conditions. Third, multitudes were saved as a result, and finally, we find great joy in the city. All of these benefits were due to the persecution of the church, even the joy. What was the city so joyous about? Not the persecution, that's for sure. The city was joyous because it had been saved, and every soul within its gates knew it.

The first hundred times I read that Scripture I thought the "scattering" was a negative thing. I thought it weakened the church. In truth, I thought the apostles were acting cowardly by running away. Nothing could be further from the truth. God intends for His people to scatter. Why? Because multitudes of people who would never have heard the Word of God heeded it and accepted it.

Even Jesus refused to remain in one place. Jesus was compelled by God to scatter. *"Now when it was day, He departed and went into a deserted place. And the crowd sought Him, and came to Him, **and tried to keep Him from leaving them**; but He said to them, 'I must preach the kingdom of God to other cities also, because of this purpose I have been sent.'"* (Luke 4:42-43) If Jesus had to scatter, so do we. Why is the scattering of the Word so important?

Please allow me to use an illustration from nature. Let's say, for example, that you have a flower that is native to your hometown or anywhere for that matter. This flower can only be found within its borders, and it is a thing of beauty. The flower propagates by producing a seed that falls to the ground at the end of the growing season. During the next season, the seeds spring up and blossom.

This flower can spread in several ways. For example, one flower may produce one seed, but each plant may contain 5 to 20 flowers. Now, as that one plant can drop up to 20 seeds on the ground, naturally the flower will spread. How long will it take for that flower to reach from your hometown (mine is in New Jersey) to say, Pennsylvania? How about Ohio, Colorado, or even California? That could take quite some time and may never make it due to improper weather and soil conditions.

Now when you factor in the wind, the seeds will spread more rapidly. It causes them to scatter. How about if the birds eat the seeds and as they are flying they drop the seeds along with their feces? Now you have the flower spreading over a much broader area, causing a more rapid expanse.

Who wants to be covered with feces to accomplish God's will? For some, believe it or not, that is their role. That is the equivalent of persecution—and especially martyrdom; however, under these conditions it may never leave the borders of North America.

What if a man catches the bird, puts it in a cage, gets on a boat or airplane and travels to Europe? Now you have that seed leaving the borders of North America. As long as the conditions are right, the moment one seed hits fertile soil that same flower will spring up and repeat the process. Understand that the seed had no inclination of traveling in this manner. It simply falls off the plant and very comfortably hits the ground. Where it goes next and how it gets there is up to God.

We see this same process in action in the above Scripture. The only difference is that Christianity is the flower, the Word of God in the apostles is the seed, and persecution is the catalyst for the scattering. Could Christianity have spread without the persecution of the church? Probably, but not nearly as fast or as far, and certainly not as effectively. When God's people are forced to scatter, it is like the birds dropping seeds everywhere. Flowers begin to pop up and reproduce wherever they are dropped.

Inertia

Why use persecution? Can't there be an easier way? In physics, there is a law that states that an object at rest will remain at rest and an object in motion will remain in motion until an external force sets it in motion, stops it, or changes its course. It is called the law of "inertia." As human beings, we seem to be subject to the spiritual side of this law. Without a catalyst, we enter into a "comfort zone" and seem to require a stiff kick in the "you know what" in order to get us out of it.

Persecution is the external force required to break our inertia. It is the force required to get us lazy-by-nature humans off our butts and into God's kingdom. In other words, without persecution you may never even consider the fact that you need God. You may not even know that you need a Savior.

Have you ever experienced something so life changing that it causes you to do something completely radical like quitting your job or packing up your stuff and moving? That could be God breaking your inertia. God intends for us to scatter. How else could we reach the lost sheep of the world? America was founded through the scattering of the English Christians and, as a result, it has since become the greatest sender of missionaries in the history of the world. Most of us would never go on our own. Here is a prime example of scattering from Scripture:

> *"Now those who were scattered **after the** persecution that arose over Stephen traveled **as far as** Phoenicia, Cyprus, and Antioch, **preaching the Word** to no one but Jews only. But some of them were men from Cyprus and Cyrene, who, when they had come to Antioch, spoke to the Hellenists, preaching the Lord Jesus. **And the hand of the Lord was with them, and a great number believed and turned to the Lord."***
> **—Acts 11:19-21**

Had the persecution not arisen, these apostles would not have been compelled to travel as far as they did. As a result of their travels, they began to come into contact with a group called the Hellenists.

These were folks who had adopted the Greek language and culture. They were primarily Jews of the Diaspora, Jews who had been dispersed to the surrounding regions from the Holy Land of Palestine after the Babylonian captivity. Many of these Jews no longer even spoke Hebrew and had, for all intents and purposes, become Greek. Without the persecution of the church and the ensuing scattering, these folks may have never been reached. The same holds true for America. God culture is unchanging.

Join the Club

There is one other major purpose for persecution. It has to do with credibility. Note the following passage:

> *"And when Saul had come to Jerusalem, **he tried to join the disciples**; but they were all afraid of him, and did not believe that he was a disciple. But Barnabas took him and brought him to the apostles. And he declared to them how he had seen the Lord on the road, and how he had preached boldly at Damascus in the name of Jesus. So he was with them at Jerusalem, coming in and going out. And he spoke boldly in the name of Jesus and disputed against the Hellenists, but they attempted to kill him. **When the brethren found out**, they brought him down to Caesarea and sent him out to Tarsus."*
>
> **—Acts 9:26-30**

It was not until there was an attempt on the life of Saul (whose name God later changed to Paul) that the brethren accepted him. Why is that? A man is not willing to die for something that he has no true belief in. I love what **Pascal**, the French philosopher and mathematician, who developed the modern theory of probability, and lived from the years 1623-1662, said, "I prefer to believe those writers who get their throats cut for what they write."

When the brethren found out that Saul was willing to die, it confirmed two things: (1) he was a true believer and (2) he has now been persecuted like us. It is like Saul immediately gained entry into the "Persecuted for Christ" club. He was now part of their culture. Not just anyone can apply for membership because the initiation ceremony may be deadly. Take heed of the result: *"Then the churches throughout all Judea, Galilee, and Samaria had peace and were edified* (which means encouraged). *And walking in the fear of the Lord and in the comfort of the Holy Spirit, **they were multiplied.*** (Acts 9:31)

The persecution will not last forever. *"For His anger is but for a moment, His favor is for life; weeping may endure for a night, but joy comes in the morning."* (Psalm 30:5)

Keep Your Word

I cannot finish this chapter without you gaining an understanding of what tribulation and persecution is and is not. You must learn how to distinguish between whether God is refining you or if you have simply made some bad mistakes. You *can* know this. The Word contains all the information you need. So let's get started.

The word "tribulation" means grievous trouble, severe trial or suffering. Tribulation is the type of trouble that causes one great grief. We are not talking about minor problems here. The word "persecution" actually means to pursue with harassing or oppressive treatment. Depending on where you live in the world, persecution may take on numerous and diverse forms and embodiments.

Let's begin with what does not qualify for persecution in relation to the kingdom of God. I believe that God has gotten a bad reputation as a result of what has been passed off as persecution, mainly due to the misunderstanding of God's nature and culture. Oftentimes, things are blamed on God that actually have nothing to do with Him. Maybe you have had this happen to you.

God is not a child abuser. God does not persecute. People persecute. God delivers. You are His child and He wants what is best for you. If I were to purposely cause one of my children pain, suffering and/or illness on purpose, the courts would put me in jail for child abuse. I would be viewed as what is perhaps the worst type of human being walking the face of the earth today. Even the prisoners would hate me. I would be considered evil, callous and unloving. Yet, many of us accuse God, who is Love, of this very same behavior on a daily basis.

With that in mind, let's begin with the topic of illness. I believe God's reputation has suffered the greatest damage as a result of human beings getting sick. God does not make you sick. Most illnesses are the aftermath of poor lifestyle habits such as drinking, smoking, overeating, stress, or quite simply the result of a germ, virus, cancer, environmental problem, and more. The lifestyle habits can be changed with a little discipline. The other items are a result of the corruption of the physical condition of the earth and its surrounding atmosphere due to the fall of man. God did not create this earth for you to be sick. Sin brought death to mankind, and death brought illness.

Death is ultimately the result of sin, but not necessarily the sin you may be thinking of. Allow me to explain. Note the following passage from the Word of God:

> "If anyone sees his brother sinning a sin **that does not lead to death,** he will ask, **and He will give him life** for those who commit sin not leading to death. **There is sin leading to death.** (The desecration of one's body, God's temple, would be an example) I do not say that he should pray about that. All unrighteousness is sin, (unrighteousness is anything that is not right with God) and there is sin not leading to death."
>
> **—1 John 5:16-17**

If an illness is due to sin, it is not God's fault. It is yours. However, not all sin causes you to become ill. In fact, I believe very little of it does. Yes, illness is a result of sin. *"And the wages of sin are death,"* (Romans 6:23), but not necessarily the sins *you* commit. Illness is a result of "original sin" which not only corrupted mankind but the entire state of our universe. You began dying the day you were born, but the Great Physician had a plan.

"For since by man came death, by Man also came the resurrection of the dead. For as in Adam all die, even so in Christ all shall be made alive."
—1 Corinthians 15:21-22

The truth is God is not putting illness *on* you; He has taken it *from* you—and not just physical illness. When you receive Him, He takes your illness, depression, grief, sorrow, fear, anxiety and, most importantly, *your sin.* Here is your proof from the Word of God:

*"But He was wounded for our transgressions, He was bruised for our iniquities, the chastisement for our peace was upon Him, and by His stripes **we are healed.**"*
—Isaiah 53:5-6

We must learn how to receive healing from our Lord. We must learn how to pull from the Word of God. God's Word is a resource that is available to any man willing to believe it, and it has the solution to every aspect of human life.

*"My son, give attention to my words, incline your ear to my sayings. Do not let them depart from your eyes; keep them in the midst of your heart; for they are life to those who find them, **and health to all their flesh.** Keep your heart with all diligence, **for out of it spring the issues of life.**"*
—Proverbs 4:20-23

If you eat fatty foods, drink like a fish, smoke like a chimney and have a heart attack, it is pretty easy to understand that you have not been persecuted, nor is it God who is the source of your illness or your tribulation. The simple fact is you have been foolish, and the only aspect of the Word that is operating fully in your life is the law of sowing and reaping. Unfortunately, all you will reap is ill health.

If you drive like an idiot, get into a car accident and become disabled, you are not experiencing tribulation for the kingdom of God; you are experiencing tribulation as a result of idiocy. If you commit adultery and lose half your "stuff" along with your family, you are not experiencing tribulation and persecution for the kingdom of God; you are simply reaping what you have sown. I think you get my point. So how can we tell if we are suffering for God? Let's allow the words of Jesus to illuminate us:

"Behold a sower went out to sow. And as he sowed, some seed fell by the wayside, and the birds of the air came and devoured them. Some fell on stony places, where they did not have much earth, and they immediately sprang up because they had no depth of earth. But when the sun was up they were scorched, and because they had no root they withered away. And some fell among thorns, and the thorns sprang up and choked them. But others fell on good ground and yielded a crop: some a hundredfold, some sixty, some thirty. He who has ears to hear, let him hear."
—Matthew 13:3-9

Before I comment on this, let's hear Jesus' explanation of the parable:

*"When **anyone** hears the Word of the kingdom, and **does not understand it**, then the wicked one comes and snatches away what was sown in his heart. This is he who received seed by the wayside. But he received seed on stony places, this is he who hears the word, and immediately receives it with joy, yet he has no root in himself, but endures only for a while. For when **tribulation** or **persecution** arises **because of the Word**, immediately he stumbles...."*
—Matthew 13:18-21

The main reason I have written this book for you is because I do not want you to fall by the wayside. I want to help you and encourage you to gain understanding. When you go to church, read your Bible, attend a revival meeting, and read this book, Satan just sits by and waits to see who has understanding—and who does not. When you get in your car, he is in the back seat listening to see if you have gained understanding. When you close your Bible, he waits to hear if you have understanding. The very second he discovers that you don't, he snatches away the Word.

Look at the world around you. The Word *is* being snatched away. The majority of the world, the church included, is deceived. I challenge you to do your own survey. Ask your friends, relatives, neighbors, co-workers about what they think of the Bible. For those who are actually believers, attempt to discern their level of understanding.

When you find out how uncommitted we as a whole group of people are to God and His Word, you will understand why we have the drug, alcohol, teenage pregnancy, adultery, fornication, rape, murder, gang, pornography and other problems that are destroying our society. The Word has been snatched from our hearts and from our culture and has been replaced with sin. Until we as a society commit to God's Word, we will continue to degrade.

I have studied several major religions and do you know what I found? The reason they do not believe in Jesus is because they do not understand God. Let's look at Islam and Judaism for example.

Our Jewish brothers and sisters have been blinded to how Jesus fulfills the Day of Atonement. They understand the concept of atonement, but they fail to recognize how Jesus fulfills the dual role of the sin offering killed upon the altar and the scapegoat that is presented alive before the Lord. He is the atoning Lamb of God that takes away the sin of the world. Jesus is the fulfillment of the covenant made with Abraham. Jesus is the end of the law.

In Islam, there is a concept of Jesus. He is even the Judge of mankind at the end of time. Imagine the irony! However, they refuse to believe that He is the Son of God, even though the Q'ran states that God impregnated Mary, which is the very definition of fatherhood. They cannot understand how God would humble Himself to become sinful flesh—or how the Almighty God could lower himself to poop and pee in His diaper. They feel that would be beneath an all-powerful God, when the truth is that it makes Him all the more powerful.

Because we have a lack of understanding as to who God is and how He operates, the devil has been able to steal the Lord from about three-fourths of mankind's heart—and that is assuming that all those professing to be Christians have understanding. The real number is probably above ninety percent. You must understand that you have been created to house the Living God.

Scientists have recently discovered through the mapping of the human genome that mankind has implanted deep within him a gene that causes you to desire God. They call it the "God gene." Of course, they try to pass it off as proof that there is no God, and that the gene causes you to desire something that isn't real. The truth is that God put it there. You were created to be one with God. When you are not, God programmed your genetic makeup to look for Him. You are like a homing pigeon, always seeking your nest.

When that connection is severed, it leaves a void within man that Satan, the "god" of this world (2 Corinthians 4:4), is more than happy to fill. His most effective tools are violence, jealousy, hatred and immorality. He fills it with pre-marital sex, corruption and war. He fills it with disbelief, false religion, pride and ego. He fills it with all of the horrors we see inflicted upon the earth in this present age.

The end result is the persecution of the righteous. The devil tries to squelch whatever Godliness is left in the world so he can reign. He wants to steal *all* of the Word, but we know the end of the book. The Lord Jesus Christ is coming to free His people of this natural world and carry us into eternity.

Find a Friend in Jesus

How can we know if we are being molded and refined by negative situations in our lives? It is simple if you just apply the Word. Jesus, in the parable of the sower, explained, *"...for when tribulation and persecution arises for the Word's sake...."* Are you experiencing trouble because of the Word? Are you being persecuted because of Jesus, and because of God culture? If you can answer yes, then you are being refined. If your answer is no, then you need to search your inner self, your behavior, and your belief system for the root cause. *It is* that simple.

In the West, you are not likely to experience the same type of persecution as in many Eastern countries. You will most likely experience slander. You may be marked as a social outcast, a weirdo, or a Jesus freak. You may even lose friends. I have, but that's okay. The Friend you will gain will always be loyal. He will never leave you nor forsake you. He will stay by your side to the bitter end. What a friend we have in Jesus! A little tribulation and persecution in the "now" goes a long way in the "forever."

— CHAPTER 4 —

Beyond a Promise

I was recently reminded of how difficult and uncomfortable it can be when meeting new people while I was securing a brand new business relationship. The difficulty lies in the unfamiliarity. There are new personalities to learn and new business cultures. Who is subordinate to whom? What's the new pecking order?

I remember walking into the room and feeling that all eyes were focused on me. Can I fulfill their expectations? What are my expectations of them? It took some time to get to know the individuals as well as the group as a whole. In the beginning, it just felt weird. I felt like I had just moved to a new school and had no friends, like I was alone at the lunch table. I'm sure you must have experienced this at some point in your life.

In time, however, I began to grow more comfortable in my new surroundings and the others became more comfortable with me. We began to get to know one another. I learned what I could and could not say and to whom. In essence, I began to build new relationships. I was learning their culture.

I recently had a friend move to a foreign country. When we last spoke he was having a very difficult time assimilating into the new culture. As I began to probe a little deeper, I learned that he was not putting forth much effort to learn the local ways and customs. More significantly, he was not making an effort to learn the language and it was prohibiting him from making friends and creating new relationships.

The new culture seemed very strange to him. People were not very direct in their communication and he could not understand why the people acted the way they did. As a result, he had been left isolated and alone. He had become a social and cultural outcast. Unless he began to engage in this new society and understand their ways, things were never going to change for him. He would be alone forever.

It is really no different when getting to know God. At first, it seems quite strange. You don't know Him and you have absolutely no idea what to expect from this newfound relationship. You do not understand His ways or His culture. In fact, you really don't even understand His language. It can be downright intimidating.

Thank God He does not make us cultural and social outcasts. He comes forth to meet us where we are and reveals His will, His ways and His love for mankind individually and as a whole. He has given us His Word so we can learn about Him, understand Him and commune with Him but we must learn to approach Him His way.

God has a culture. He has implemented a specific set of rules that we must follow when approaching Him. His ways are ancient and so is His culture. Unlike man, God is not progressive. He is unchanging. As a result, we have had a continuous misunderstanding of Him, an ongoing generation gap if you will.

At first, as you are learning His ways, He will be quite lax with them. As your relationship grows, He will begin to require more from you. He will begin to invite you to participate in His Life. He will require you to get to know His ways, His Word, and His essence, but you must do it His way.

All too often, however, we are unwilling to engage with Him in His way. We want it to be our way so we begin to mold Him into *our* image. We begin to turn God into who *we* want Him to be and who we *think* He should be. We turn Him into a religion. Blaise Pascal once said, "Men never do evil so completely and cheerfully as when they do it from religious conviction." I believe he was right.

We make up all kinds of silly doctrines, theologies and rituals. We try to get God to approach us as opposed to us approaching Him. Just like my friend that moved, we refuse to learn His ways, His culture and His language. Therefore we never gain entrance into His kingdom. Then we are surprised when things begin to fall apart and God does not turn out to be who we thought He was. So we discard Him all together. To make matters even worse, we begin to take out our frustration upon mankind. In the words of Anne Lamott, "You know you've created God in your own image when it turns out that God hates all the same people you do."

An Ancient Practice

By now you are well aware that that is not God's will for your life and it may be that you are not even sure how to begin interacting with God. Perhaps you haven't spoken to Him for a while or maybe you never have. So where do we begin? It's not as if you can just knock on His door, is it? Let's take a closer look at God culture and learn how we can begin interacting with our Creator.

God's culture is one of covenant and it is the foundation for comprehending how He thinks, acts and operates. Even more importantly, it is the primary source of your relationship with Him. Nothing, not even miracles, occurs outside of the principle we are about to discuss. Everything that transpires between you and God will operate according to it. It is the way God deals with mankind, and it is the way God redeemed mankind. Ancient cultures have understood, negotiated, and transacted their livelihoods for millennia according to this principle but it is something modern man knows very little about. Covenant is God's modus operandi. It is His method of operation. Covenant is the chief cornerstone of God culture.

In the West, we have all but lost this ancient practice. In fact, if I were to ask you to define "covenant," the word "promise" would most likely be the concept you would describe to me. Although a covenant is a type of promise, there is much more to it. A covenant goes **beyond a promise.**

Our concept of a promise is only binding upon one party. I promise to do something for you, or you promise to do something for me. This is where our greatest misunderstanding of God occurs. We expect God to form a unilateral contract with us, meaning He has all of the responsibility and we retain none for ourselves. All too often we want to receive His goodness with no strings attached. When we do promise something to God, we never truly bind ourselves to it. So in essence, it has no real meaning. I regret to inform you that God does not operate in that manner. That is not His culture.

God's way is to make a bilateral contract with you, which is binding upon two parties. This dual responsibility is what distinguishes a covenant from a promise. All throughout the Scriptures we see the concept of "If you, then I," employed by God. In other words, God acts when you act. This is what it means to step out in faith. Faith is acting before you know the outcome. In the movie *Hope Floats*, the character played by Sandra Bullock stated, "Faith is believing in something when common sense tells you not to." In part, she was right but faith is no longer blind when it is based upon covenant.

Grow Up

Allow me to illustrate these two different contractual concepts through an example most of us can relate to. As parents, we promise our children that we will take care of them. We, the parents, have a responsibility to uphold, but the child absorbs none. They simply wait for us to feed them, clothe them, educate them, and more. If that is as far as your relationships with your children go, you will end up with selfish and self-serving children who never learn to stand on their own two feet and who never learn to accept responsibility as mature adults. This can also be the case with your relationship to God if you act similarly in your role as a child of the Father and never move "beyond a promise" and into covenant with Him.

So how do parents overcome this? We begin by giving our children chores. As they progress in age and maturity, we oblige them to take on more responsibility. This prepares them to assume the role of an adult as they enter the job market. It also prepares them to raise and support a family of their own. This is how your relationship with God begins as well—with trust. First a little is given, then more and more. As time goes by, your relationship continues to progress.

You must learn to trust that God will perform what He says He will, and He must confirm that you will be faithful to the small responsibilities, or chores, He entrusts to you. Just as you give more responsibility to your children as they mature, God gives *you* more responsibility as you mature. Moving "beyond a promise" is a process, just as growing up and maturing is a process. Keep in mind: unlike the physical growth process, which just happens, you must understand your covenant relationship with God in order to progress in it. It must be a conscious and purposeful choice. It does not just happen. You have a cultural responsibility to work at it.

When you enter into a covenant relationship with someone, *both* parties must be willing and bound to accept, at minimum, as great a responsibility as the adjoining party. If you give one hundred dollars, I must do the same. If you pledge your house, I must at minimum pledge mine. If you give your life, I must be willing to give mine. The culture of covenant requires trust and responsibility between those entering into the covenant.

Historically, the most binding of covenants are sealed in blood. The parties in covenant would actually make small incisions in their wrists, for example, and inter-mingle their blood with one another. Thus the blood covenant would be sealed. Each party would have the other's blood running through their veins.

I Promise

To understand this in accordance to our relationship with God, we must understand covenant in Scripture. Although the Word of God contains various covenants, the basis of both the Old and New Testaments is the covenant "cut" between Abraham and El Shaddai. It is not just the basis for Christianity. It is the basis of Judaism, Christianity and Islam, the three major world religions.

To discover the truth, let's begin with the *promises* God made to Abram.

> *"Now the Lord said to Abram, 'Get out of your country, from your family and from your father's house; to a land that I will show you. I will make you a great nation; I will bless you and make your name great; and you shall be a blessing. I will bless those who bless you, and I will curse him who curses you. And in you all of the families of the earth shall be blessed.' So Abram departed as the Lord had spoken to him..."*
> **—Genesis 12:1-4**

I must reiterate that God has not yet covenanted with Abram (Abraham). He has simply made several promises in order to invite Abram into a relationship with Him. Please realize that God knows Abram... completely. He knows everything about Abram but, at this point, Abram does not know anything about God. In order to build a relationship with Abram, God proactively promises to fulfill both Abram's needs and desires, just as *you* would help another person whose trust you were hoping to gain. Missionaries have operated according to this principle for centuries, probably since the Book of Acts.

It will also behoove you to note how Abram progresses "beyond a promise" as *your* relationship with God will follow this same pattern. Until you have an understanding of the culture of covenant, your relationship with God and your ability to function according to His way of doing things will be severely limited. This is why Christian people continually report that it becomes more and more difficult to receive from God over time. Nearly one hundred percent of the time they are puzzled by this, and sometimes give up as a result. It is not that God has rescinded His promises. It is simply that He was offering and giving to you so as to invite you into His presence and into a relationship with Him.

When it feels like He stops giving to you, it is a sign that God is prodding you forward to do your part in the relationship. You have stopped progressing. There is a cultural divide. This disrupts the collaborative development of the alliance. Figuratively speaking, you are looking for God in a place He no longer dwells. He has put the ball in your court and because you still have your hand out you have unknowingly been left behind. In essence, it is your move and God will not move until you do. He has already fulfilled His promise and now it is time to fulfill yours. It is time to move on to the next task – together in a spirit of unity with the Father.

To make matters worse, you have become like a spoiled child, only willing to take from your parents and never willing to give. You have become like an unaccountable adolescent who is completely unwilling to step up and accept responsibility. Therefore, it is *we* who limit how much responsibility God can give us. Not God. If you think about this, it sounds much more like American culture than God culture.

Take note of the roots of the word "response-ability." It is always your response that determines how much of God's ability He will entrust you with. That is what "response-ability" is. It is your ability to respond.

If you have found yourself in this position, do not be discouraged. Simply move forward. The fact that God is not doing everything for you is actually a sign that He has begun to trust you. He has given you responsibility. Rejoice in this and begin taking the actions that the Lord has placed upon your heart. This is how you continue growing in your covenant relationship with Him. If you would like to enter into a "forever" relationship with God, you must enter into covenant with Him just like Abraham did—and God changed the world through Abraham. He can do the same through you too.

Small Beginnings

Now that God has gotten Abram's attention through the promise He made, let's begin to examine God's cultivation of the covenant relationship He wants to establish with Abram. Our journey begins in Genesis 12, just after Abram leaves the land of Haran along with his wife, his nephew Lot, and all of their acquired servants, and enters the land of Canaan. Keep in mind that Abram is seventy-five years old when this period of his life begins. When God is at work, your age is irrelevant. If you are willing, God is always able to use you.

> *"Then the Lord appeared to Abram and said, 'To your descendants I will give this land.' And there he built an altar to the Lord, who had appeared to him. And he moved from there to the mountain east of Bethel, and he pitched his tent with Bethel on the West and Ai on the East; there he built an altar to the Lord **and called on the name of the Lord.** So Abram journeyed, going on still toward the south."*
> **—Genesis 12:7-9**

Since the topic of discussion here is covenant, I will not get into the boundaries of the "promised land." It is relevant to note, however, that God began this relationship by continually revealing himself to Abram. Each time He does, Abram learns a little more about who God is, how He operates, and what God is attempting to accomplish through him. That is what revelation is. It is God opening Himself up or revealing Himself and His plans to you. The question is: Are you responding? Are you learning about Him on a continual basis? Through the power of the Holy Spirit, the Word of God, prayer and worship, you should be having the same experience in your life as Abram.

Secondly, we find that Abram's initial responses to God are faith, obedience, and action, immediately expressed in worship. We will spend much more time on these concepts later, but it is imperative to note that your relational response to God must begin the same way. This is how we prove ourselves to God.

Every covenant, just like any other contract, has binding agreements. God's binding agreements are those stated immediately above: faith, obedience and action. Do not take these lightly. They are easy to give lip service to but very difficult to perform. When pressure comes, will you uphold your end? Will you have faith, believe, obey and do?

You may be thinking…sometimes yes, sometimes no, I won't. To do so requires a certain amount of "extremism" at times. God's people always have been and always will be considered a bit extreme. When kept in the proper context of God culture, it simply means extremely dedicated believers holding themselves accountable to the ways of the Lord. That's a good thing.

The question is, how "radical" are you willing to be? How far are you willing to go? Adhering to the ways of God under pressure and scrutiny can sometimes feel like they are more easily said than done. *"These people draw near to me with their mouths and honor me with their lips, but have removed their hearts far from Me."* (Isaiah 29: 13)

Written some five thousand five hundred years ago this may be the first historical record of people merely paying "lip service" to someone. How ironic is it that the "someone" happens to God? I guess some things never change. You may also find that sometimes you make exceptions to the covenant required to follow God's ways as well. Thank God that He is merciful.

As you will see this was not the case with Abraham. He went all the way. As you experience God culture, you will soon find that it is *your* actions that determine God's actions in your life. That is the true definition of responsibility within the kingdom of God. Therefore, understand that the concept of covenant is not just important; it can literally be the difference between spiritual life and death. It also reflects the level of commitment you are willing to make and whether you are willing to keep and respect the covenant with God.

Thirdly, you must *obey* the Word of God, which instructs you to accept God's sacrifice. Finally, since all you know at this beginning point is that God is willing to save you, you must begin to worship Him. Then, by mingling worship with prayer, you invite God to begin communicating with you. Communication is not only how *any* relationship begins, it is also what causes each one to grow and mature. Communication is one of the foundations of any culture, and God culture is certainly no exception.

Take careful note of the following sequence of events and understand that *God knows our frame.* (Psalm 103:14) He recognizes our imperfections and our fears. He will always be faithful to us, even when we screw up, which for those of you who are like me and, as you will soon find out, like Abram as well, can be quite often.

As Abram enters Egypt, he believes that the Egyptians are going to kill him and steal his wife. Obviously he does not understand God's power or plan yet. So he instructs his wife to lie and say that she is his sister. In actuality, it was only a half lie. Sound familiar? She actually *is* his *half-*sister. You would think that God would cut him off at this point and go find someone better suited for the job. This man is obviously full of iniquity and sin.

In truth, before we meet Christ, we are all in the same condition. Abram simply does not know any better yet, and neither will you until you begin relating with Christ. It's like traveling to a foreign country. The first time you go, you are culturally lost. Learning God culture, however, is a process that takes an entire lifetime. There was only one perfect Man in history and the rest of us are under perpetual construction. Therefore, it is okay for you to love who you are right now and who you become as you evolve. God created you to be that way.

Because He loves and understands you, He will be very patient with you as long as you continue to seek Him. We get into trouble when we stop progressing with God, when we forsake our end of the bargain—the covenant. God can and will work with you even when you sin. That is what Jesus died for. He cannot and will not work with hypocrisy and/or apathy.

If you are willing to acknowledge that God is God, as well as your own shortcomings, God will always remain faithful to you. However, if you refuse to even acknowledge Him, He will refuse to acknowledge you. (Luke 12:9) He will still love you and wait for you to seek Him again, but *you* will have severed the connection. Not God.

"'Please say that you are my sister, that it will be well with me for your sake, and that I may live because of you.' So it was, when Abram came into Egypt, that the Egyptians saw the woman, that she was very beautiful. The princes of Pharaoh also saw her and commended

her to Pharaoh. And the woman was taken to Pharaoh's house...But the Lord plagued Pharaoh and his house with great plagues because of Sarai..."

—Genesis 12:13-17

God had a plan for these two folks, and there was no way he was going to allow a little imperfection, or Pharaoh, to mess it up. Take this to heart. You *will* mess up from time to time, but God will not give up on you as long as you keep your heart in the right place. This is what covenant is all about. However, God will not baby you forever. He will require you to take responsibility for your life. It is imperative that you move "beyond a promise" and into covenant with Him. At this point of our discussion, however, Abram is at the beginning of his relationship with God. He still has a long way to go. As you will soon discover, God is patient. He will continue working on and with Abram as long as Abram allows Him.

Do you remember a little earlier when God promised to bless Abram if Abram would just be obedient to Him? God will always perform His Word. Here is the manifestation of the blessing to Abram:

"Abram was very rich in livestock, in silver, and in gold...Now the land was not able to support them (Abram and Lot), *that they might dwell together, for their possessions were so great that they could not dwell together..."*

—Genesis 13:2 and 6

God never does anything halfway. It is not part of His culture. If you are willing to obey Him, He will bless you. Blessing Abraham beyond measure is how He gained Abram's trust. Providing for your family, or by some other means that is important to you, may be how He gains your trust as well.

Keep on Keepin' On

God never stops there. God is complete and He always finishes His projects. Unfortunately, we oftentimes do not and instead stop short of the finish line. It seems that we have this belief that the kingdom of God is all about our blessing. We have a tendency to think about the blessing as being the end of our faith when in reality it is merely the beginning.

We will now see God begin to move Abram "beyond a promise" and into a covenant relationship with Him. This is a critical time between God and Abram. God is about to confirm what Abram is made of, and *Abram is about to find out what Abram is made of* as well. We all must expect to go through this time of trial when entering the kingdom of God.

Refinement is a part of God culture. It is imperative for God to test and mold our character. God already knows everything about us. However, in order to improve, we must learn about our own shortcomings when experiencing difficult situations. Acknowledging our weaknesses allows God to correct us, thus leading to the growth of our relationship with Him. *"And He said to me, 'My grace is sufficient for you, for My strength is made perfect in weakness.'"* (2 Corinthians 12:9) It is also how we tap into the power of God.

God will walk with you as far as you are willing to go…and then some. He does not tire and He never runs out of strength. This is why it is so important for you to understand the concept of covenant. When you know that you are His partner and that *He will never leave you nor forsake you* (Hebrews 13:5), your possibilities become endless. Why? Because *He* is endless! Let's observe the Lord in action.

El Shaddai

> *"After these things, the word of the Lord came to Abram in a vision, saying, 'Do not be afraid, Abram. I am your shield* (I am El Shaddai), *your exceedingly great reward.'"*
> **—Genesis 15:1**

Do you remember how rich God made Abram? He and Lot had so much "stuff" that they could not even remain in the same land. Yet God does not state that the riches are Abram's reward. God says that HE is Abram's not just great but *exceedingly* great reward. This means that God is a reward that is sufficient beyond the greatest riches you can possibly imagine. Realization of His magnitude is unattainable.

The word "exceedingly" means to an unusually extreme degree. God is the greatest reward you can have in your life. He is unusual beyond anything that exists in the universe. Stop looking only at His hands and what is in them. Begin to seek His face and His will. If your children only looked at your hands, or more specifically, at the wallet in them, you would consider them to be incredibly rude and manipulative. You would still love them but you would also realize that, as their parent, you need to teach them to love, respect and honor you.

Me, Me, Me

Is your relationship to God any different than that of a child's to a parent? Are you still trying to manipulate Him? This is exactly how children act. We will now see that this is the precise stage that Abram is at with God. We all come to this point in our early walk with Jehovah. Unfortunately, many of us never progress beyond it. Be encouraged if you recognize this as your stage with God. Recognition is the key to entering God culture. Whenever you do decide to commit to Him, He will never disappoint you. Let's see how God moves Abram forward in the relationship.

> "'But,' Abram said, 'Lord God, **what will You give me,** seeing I go childless, and the heir of my house is Eliezer of Damascus?' Then Abram said, 'Look, you have given me no offspring; one born in my house is my heir.'"
> **—Genesis 15:2-3**

The above statement from Abram is very telling as to where he is with God. What we see, especially in regard to the tone of his request, is a selfish and manipulative child. Being childless in ancient times was equated with being accursed. Since God has promised to bless him, and give him no part of a curse, Abram has everything a man could want with the exception of one very significant "item" – a child to inherit that which

God has blessed him. Thus Abram's request: "God, what will you give me? You know, Lord…I still have no offspring. I am still cursed."

Just like every child, Abram feels it is all about him at this point. Abram has not yet progressed to the level of covenant. He is still at the early point of a one-way promise with God where he believes that only God has any responsibilities to uphold. He is still in the "unilateral" phase of his spirituality. This is all about to change. Abram is progressing, but God still has some work to do on him. He is solidly in the "promise" phase of his life with God, but he is quickly pressing toward "covenant." God has a way to expedite this move. God *will* bring him into a bilateral relationship. Let's watch God in action.

Is That Possible?

> *"And behold, the Word of the Lord came to him saying, 'This one shall not be your heir, but one who will come from your own body shall be your heir.' Then he brought him outside and said, 'Look now toward heaven, and count the stars if you can number them.' And He said to him, 'So shall your descendants be.' And he believed in the Lord, and He accounted it to him for righteousness."*
> **—Genesis 15:4-6**

In order to truly understand why God does what He does here, you must realize that God has just promised Abram something that is not humanly possible. Believe it or not, that is part of God culture as well. In fact, that's when you know you are smack in the middle of it! He has just promised a seventy-five year-old man with a sixty-five year-old wife who has been barren her entire life, and who is well past menopause, "the age of child bearing," that they will have a child. Amazingly enough, Abram believed Him! Because of this belief of God, not belief *in* God (most people believe *in* God, but very few actually believe God), God declares Abram righteous, which simply means in right standing with Him. Faith will always put you in right standing with God. It will always cause God to act. Faith is the *"if you"* portion followed by the *"then I"* of God's covenant.

The problem with faith, however, is that if you do not continue to feed it, it will die. This is the downfall of many good-hearted people today. Have you ever noticed how excited you can be about a project when it is new? What happens as time goes by, especially if it does not appear to be going so well? The enthusiasm begins to wane, doesn't it? Why do you think this happens? The answer is that you begin to lose your faith in it. The vision begins to fade. If you do not keep that vision firmly implanted in your psyche with the end goal in mind, it will die and you will eventually give up and fail.

Faith works the same way. If you do not feed your faith by studying the Word of God daily, worshipping and praying continually, and stepping out and into the power of God, your faith will eventually weaken and perhaps even die. However, God has the solution for Abram. Since *God is unchanging* (Malachi 3:6), this will also work for you.

He instructs Abram to look up at the night sky and attempt to number the stars. In the world we live in, we cannot even see the majority of the stars that are visible to the naked eye. We simply have too much light pollution. This was not the case in Abram's time. The only obstacles to seeing the night sky were the few torches that were burning.

Remember, Abram is not even in the city at this point. He is in the Valley of Shaveh, getting ready to bring his people home after delivering them from capture. The sky would have been utterly ablaze with stars. One would not even need to begin counting to realize that numbering all of these stars is futile. God informs Abram that his descendants will be of a similar multitude.

Also note that Abram would have spent much more time outdoors than today's modern man does. I realized not too long ago that we rarely even look at the night sky anymore. I remember being a child and lying on my front lawn staring up at the night sky in awe and wonder. I then realized that I have not done that in nearly thirty years! This was simply not the case with the ancients. They did not have televisions, computers, and all of the gadgets that keep us from nature. Even books, or scrolls, were rare. What they had, though, was imagination.

We have a saying in America, "Out of sight, out of mind." It simply means that if something is not directly before your eyes, you will almost immediately forget about it. This truth is the death of faith. It is the death of God culture. That is why it is imperative to keep God, His Word, His promises and His covenant continually before your eyes. It keeps you in faith. God could not allow Abram to fall prey to "out of sight, out of mind." So what did He do? He chose an image, which is the root word of imagination, that He knew Abram could not escape from—the stars.

Every time Abram looked up at night, he saw his future descendants. Every time he stepped out of his tent door, he saw his future descendants. Night after night after night he did this for twenty-four years until the image became as real and as alive to Abram as the people who stand before you every day of your life.

Did you know that God is the creator of the principle of autosuggestion? Autosuggestion is simply a means of programming your subconscious mind by bombarding it daily with the images of who you want to become. Napoleon Hill did not create this principle—God did.

What image of faith have you put before your eyes day after day and night after night? I regret to inform you that if it is the images of the television, and let's face it we are all guilty in this regard, you will not build the faith required to cause God's will to come to pass in your life. I'm not against television; it's just that we have substituted a box that has become a major influence, some may even say idol, in our lives for God. We keep the evening news, sit-coms, re-runs of sit-coms, TV dramas, soap operas and other programs before our eyes religiously and continually. We schedule our lives around the television programming lineup.

Yet our Bibles remain sealed and gathering dust, thus rendering the Word of God powerless when your every hope, dream and desire is contained within the pages of this closed book. If you want to develop the faith of Abraham, begin by filling your eyes—which will fill your mind—and in turn fill your heart with the Word of God. This small but crucial commitment will unlock the power that created the entire universe in your life. That is how God began with Abraham. It is how He must also begin with you. Let's see how this minor alteration shifted Abraham's entire paradigm, thus unlocking the power that changed his entire destiny.

Father of Many Nations

> *"When Abram was ninety-nine years old, the Lord appeared to Abram and said... 'My covenant is with you, and you shall be a father of many nations. No longer shall your name be called Abram, but your name shall be Abraham; for **I have made you** a father of many nations.'"*
>
> **—Genesis 17:1 and 5**

You may be thinking, "What's with the name change?" Our confusion resides in the fact that in most cultures today your name does not really mean anything. Your name was probably chosen either because your parents were fond of someone bearing it or they simply liked the sound of it. Maybe it rhymes with your last name or something.

This is not the case with God culture. In Abraham's day, your name was your identity. It described who you were, who your family was, and it may even have described your physical appearance and/or personality. When you introduced yourself, you were telling your newfound acquaintance a great deal about your identity.

So God renames Abram "Abraham", which means "father of many nations." At first glance, this seems a bit peculiar because Abraham not only doesn't have any children but he is ninety-nine years old. His wife is eighty-nine and still barren. Yet every time Abraham meets someone, he declares, "Hello, I'm the father of many nations!" Sounds insane, right? It would be if God were not involved, but He is, so it's not.

By the way, God stuck His own name right in the middle of Abram's name, which is revealing in its own right. God's desire is to be one with you and for Him to actually be a part of you. This is what your redemption is all about. This is what being filled with the Holy Spirit is all about. It is not a matter of speaking in tongues or performing miracles. That is simply a means to an end. The end goal for God is to be joined together with you for eternity. Every time Abraham identified himself to another human being, he introduced that person to the God of the universe.

The Lord's name is Y-(ah)-Weh. He turned Abram's name to Abr-(ah)-am. He in turn did the same for Sarai, changing her name to Sar-(ah). This seemingly insignificant alteration assured that Jehovah remained the central figure of this arrangement, thus assuring the power of His will in coming to pass.

What was God doing? He was flooding Abraham's senses. He was changing his thought process and his culture. God was keeping His promise on the lips of Abraham. He was activating the spiritually creative power of the words we continually speak. This is an important concept. By changing Abram's name to Abraham, Abraham could not waiver. Every time he spoke it, it lined up with the promise of God.

We would be well served to heed this concept. One reason the promises of God do not come to pass in our lives is our continued wavering. One day we speak the promise, the next day we speak the curse. As James, the brother of Jesus, commented in his great New Testament oration, we become *like a ship tossed back and forth by the sea* and thus we receive nothing from the Lord.

In addition, God was keeping His promise in the ears of Abraham. He was keeping His promise in the mind of Abraham, and He was keeping His promise before the eyes of Abraham. Every time someone called his name, he heard the promise of God. Every time he said his name, he spoke the promise of God. Every time he looked up at night, he *saw* the promise of God and every time he closed his eyes at night he remembered the promise of God. With all this being done in the name of the Lord, it brought the power of God to pass. Abraham was continually being filled with faith. God became the cultural center of Abraham's world.

How Do You Know?

Although everything seems to be going well, things are not always as easy as they appear. Abraham is about to make a major blunder that will affect mankind even to this day. Let's retrace our steps just a bit and discover that "now vs. forever" also has a dark side.

"Then He said to him, 'I am the Lord who brought you out of the Ur of the Chaldeans, to give you this land to inherit it.' And he said, 'Lord God, how shall I know that I will inherit it?'"
—Genesis 15: 7-8

This is actually a very interesting question, and it is one that we ask God all the time. In essence, Abraham is asking God for confirmation. Haven't you done the very same thing? You've prayed, God spoke and gave you direction, and you said, "How will I know?" or, "God, was that really you?"

In fact, in all of my years of ministering, this is without a doubt, in one form or another, the most common and potentially crippling question people ask. It usually takes the following form: "Brother John, how can I tell if it's God who is speaking to me?" Believe it or not, the answer is quite simple. Enter into an intimate relationship with Jesus Christ, learn the Word of God, listen for **His voice only** which will be based upon the Word of God, and you will know.

Jesus said, *"…he calls his own sheep by name and leads them out. And when he brings out his own sheep, he goes before them, and the sheep follow him, **for they know his voice**. Yet they will by no means follow a stranger, but will flee from him, for they do not know the voice of strangers."*
—John 10: 4-5

You must follow Jesus intimately to know His voice. He is our advocate before the Father so allow Him to go before you. He will always lead you down the right path, in the direction of your dream, granted that it lines up with God's will. A shepherd spends so much time with his sheep leading and directing them that the sheep actually learn to recognize his voice and his voice alone. They trust only him. If you were to show up, the sheep would realize that you are not their shepherd and that your voice is unfamiliar. They will not follow you.

You must treat the Lord in this same manner. You must *learn* to recognize His voice. This begins with following Him in the small things and, more often than not, it requires making mistakes. God, who is one and the same with Jesus Christ, will not even ask you to make a major decision until you have learned to recognize His voice. He will not move you forward until you begin to assimilate into His culture.

Small mistakes result in small amounts of damage. God understands this even better than you do. God uses these mistakes to teach you the difference between His voice and a stranger's voice. Unfortunately, we humans learn more by making mistakes than by succeeding. Therefore, you must follow Him intimately. What pleases Him most is when you enter into a covenant relationship with Him. If you are willing to do this, you will never have to ask, "God, was that really you?" You'll already know.

When Abraham asked God, "How will I know?" God responds with the following, *"Bring me a three year-old heifer, a three year-old female goat, a three year-old ram, a turtledove, and a young pigeon."* (Genesis 15: 9) On the surface, this appears to be a strange request. God's response to Abraham's question was, "bring me some animals." How can this possibly bring confirmation to Abram?

> *"Then he brought all these to Him and cut them in two… Now when the sun was going down, a deep sleep fell upon Abram… And it came to pass, when the sun went down and it was dark, that behold there appeared a smoking oven and a burning torch that passed between those pieces. On the same day the Lord made a covenant with Abram…"*
> **—Genesis 15: 12 & 17-18**

Remember that Abraham lived in a culture that relied on covenant for sustenance and protection. He was extremely familiar with what God was doing. The sacrifice of the animals was exactly the confirmation that Abraham needed. It was the beginning of the covenant that changed the world forever. In truth, God was saying, "My covenant is your guarantee."

This still holds true for us today. The New Covenant that was cut with the body and blood of Jesus Christ is your guarantee as well.

> Check this out. *"On the same day the Lord made a covenant with Abram saying: 'To your descendants I have given this land, from the river of Egypt to the great river Euphrates- the Kenites, the Kennezzites… and the Jebusites.' Now Sarai, Abram's wife had born him no children…*
> **—Genesis 15:18-21 and 16:1**

From the period at the end of the sentence in Genesis 15:21, to the letter "N" in the word "now" in Genesis 16:1; we are propelled ten years into the future. Abram has been looking at the stars for ten long years. He has believed God for ten long years…and still no baby!

Did I Do That?
The very next decision Abram makes will have effects that we are still feeling today, some six thousand or so years later.

> *"Now Sarai, Abram's wife, had borne him no children. And she had an Egyptian maidservant whose name was Hagar. So Sarai said to Abram, 'See now, the Lord has restrained me from bearing children. Please, go in to my maid; perhaps I shall obtain children by her.' And Abram heeded the voice of Sarai. Then Sarai, Abram's wife, took Hagar her maid, the Egyptian, and gave her to her husband Abram to be his wife, after Abram had dwelt ten years in the land of Canaan… And the Angel of the Lord said to her, 'Behold you are with child, and you shall bear a son. You shall call his name Ishmael… He shall be a wild man; his hand shall be against every man….'"*
> **—Genesis 16:1-3 & 11**

Old Abraham didn't put up much of an argument, did he? I can still see the smoke coming off his sandals as he was running into Hagar's quarters. In all seriousness though, what actually happened here is not much different than what happened between Adam and Eve in the Garden of Eden. Abram allowed Sarai to lead, and Sarai misinterpreted God's will. In essence, she was deceived. Abram, however, just like Adam, was not deceived. He was just rebellious.

What was the root cause of this disobedience? Was it disbelief? It could not have been…the Word says that Abram believed God. He even got confirmation from God. Remember the part above where God says in so many words, "Bring me some animals"? Could it have been impatience? I don't think so. Abram had been patient for ten years. Why stop now? Then what actually was the cause of Abram's most notorious decision of sleeping with Sarai's maid?

The answer is simple. Abram had not entered into covenant with God yet. God cut the covenant. He made the offer. Abram simply had not yet accepted His invitation, and God will never force it upon anyone. Therefore, Abram did not understand that there was no way that God would ever break His promise. As a result, he may have felt that God reneged in His deal. He simply did not know God well enough. He did not understand God culture. He wasn't "all in" yet. How about you? Are you all in? Personally, I'm trying, but I still see a lot of Abram in myself. There is a consequence to only going halfway. Let's observe the aftermath of futilely attempting to complete God's plan according to our own plan, and not His.

It is interesting to note that we see God's definition of marriage in Genesis 16. The Scripture says that Sarai gave her maid Hagar to be Abram's wife. It's not that there was some glorious ceremony involved. It is the act of sexual intercourse that constitutes marriage in the eyes of God. It is the two momentarily coming together as one flesh. Once again, this is the issue with adultery. Most men have no idea that the act of adultery constitutes the covenant of marriage in the eyes of the Lord.

God's way is for the man to be the spiritual head of his household. Just like Adam, Abram should have taken control of the situation and immediately ended this foolishness. Taking authority does not mean that he is to oppress his wife. It means that he is to lead her by listening to and valuing her opinion, while making the difficult household decisions when the two cannot come to an agreement. Her role is to be a helper to him. It's not to seize control of the household.

In most cases when the man's authority is subjugated by the woman, it is usually the result of spiritual weakness on the part of the man and the result is utter chaos. We see this proven continuously within our modern cultures and families. Children who grow up in fatherless households, either through divorce or through men abandoning their responsibilities as fathers, are much more likely to participate in drug and alcohol abuse, premarital sex, and other destructive behaviors.

As a man, if you have abandoned your spiritual responsibility, next time you see your family rebelling, take a look in the mirror and like Steve Irkle from the old television sit-com *Family Matters*, say to yourself, "Did I do that?" Conversely, fathers who accompany their children to church have an 80% retention rate of their children remaining in the church as adults versus 20% when the mother alone is the sole spiritual guide.

The result of Abram's spiritual abdication was the birth of Ishmael. If you are wondering why this is significant, Abram's son Ishmael has a dreadfully notorious descendant born in the fifth century AD, who is still affecting the twenty-first century Western world. His name is Mohammed, and he is the founder and "prophet" of a now familiar religion called Islam.

Much of the trouble we experience in the world today is a result of the disobedience, selfishness, and failure on Abram's part to actually enter into covenant with God. It is a result of the immaturity and irresponsibility of a man whom God had given a tremendous amount of responsibility. He had plenty of time to grow up. But just like you and me, he was not quite sure if he could fully trust the integrity of the Almighty. So he held on to himself a little too tightly, and the result was a child born of the flesh when God's intention was to give him a child born of His Spirit.

Examine for a moment how this blunder has snowballed throughout history. Abram's concubine Hagar, whom we now know to be his true second wife by God's definition, bore Ishmael. Mrs. Ishmael in later generations bore Mohammed. Mohammed bore Islam. Islam later bore Osama Bin Laden. Osama Bin Laden bore Al Qaeda...and Al Qaeda in conjunction with radical Islam bore 9/11 and the vast majority of today's wars, genocides, and acts of terror.

Terrorism is the result of good intentions run amuck. The result of a six thousand year old decision is war in the years 2000 and beyond. You may never know the impact of both the Godly and ungodly decisions you make every day of your life. As you move forward "beyond a promise" of God and into covenant with Him, you begin to obtain the wisdom of God. If we are going to change the culture of the world, we must do it through Godly wisdom and obedience to the guidance of the Holy Spirit. You may have never thought about it, or thought about it like this before, but the future of the world is depending on us! You too have the opportunity to bring forth prosperity or destruction with the decisions you make every day.

But don't condemn old Abraham. We do exactly the same thing on a smaller scale nearly every day of our lives when we hold ourselves back from God. Abram had no idea of the enormity of his mistake. He never lived to see it. More than one billion Muslims are living in deception away from Christ as a result of Abram's seemingly small lapse in judgment. Of the twenty-three military conflicts taking place at the time of this writing, twenty of them not only involve Islam but have been provoked by Islam, the descendants of Ishmael, the *"wild man whose hands shall be against every man"* (Genesis 16:11). Just like Abram, you may never live to see the fruit of your judgmental faux pas. How many "Ishmael's" have *we* created?

Serious Business

We are about to see that it is time for Abraham to get serious. After this last blunder, God has had just about enough. The stakes are becoming too great to continue fooling around, and God is about to challenge Abraham. Remember when I told you that God's people are a bit extreme? The Lord is about to mandate a cultural decree that I must admit is a bit over the top. Both God and Abraham are about to get radical.

Notice the change in God's tone in the following passage. The Lord needs to accomplish something, and He needs to find out whether Abraham is His man or not. In chapter one, we saw that God had to place

Joseph into the necessary situations required to bring His plan to pass. We are now about to experience a similar situation in the life of Abraham. The only exception is that where Joseph had no choice, the following situations *require* choice. Covenant relationships always require the participants to voluntarily participate. We will see shortly how this principle also applies to you.

> *"And God said to Abraham: 'As for you, **you shall keep My covenant,** you and your descendants after you throughout their generations.'"*
> **—Genesis 17:9**

Allow me a little poetic license here. I would like to translate this into modern English. I think those of you who are parents like me will find this discourse all too familiar. I will use the vernacular of my very own father: "Boy, I don't care what other people do. As long as you live in *my* house, you will obey *my* rules." I am one hundred percent sure that if you have, or have ever had, a teenager, you have heard yourself utter these very words. This is pretty much the stage of spiritual life Abraham is in. He is a spiritual adolescent and God is now declaring to Abraham that it is time to grow up.

I can really empathize with what God is feeling. There are certainly times in the life of any parent when they wonder if their children will ever have the ability to stand on their own two feet. Especially when they are, let's say, about fifteen or sixteen years old and they continuously either get into or cause trouble. They look like men and women but act like children. As a result, they continually frustrate their parents, and eventually you hear yourself saying, "This is not up for debate. Just do it!"

What your child does next determines how much responsibility you will give them going forward. It is no longer time for childish mistakes. Their future is beginning to wane in the balance, and perhaps even tough love is called for at this point.

I have a very dear friend who actually had to put his child out of the house. Praise God; at the time of this writing, the son, his father, and I had spent the prior two weeks praying together in the morning. His father's tough love along with the conviction of the Holy Spirit caused this young man to repent. This was not easy for his father. It was the most excruciating thing this man and his wife have ever had the misfortune to endure, and the battle raged for six long months. Yet the child's father and mother in all their suffering could not give in. To do so would have destroyed his future. After six months, the young man came back. It was love that caused repentance, the parent's love, and even more importantly, God's love.

This is precisely the stage of spiritual life that Abraham is in at this point of our discussion. It is time to "put up or shut up." God is announcing to Abraham that if he truly desires God and he is willing to accept the blessings God bestows upon him, Abraham's partaking of this covenant is no longer optional and requires immediate action. Abraham's *choice* lies in his willingness to obey. If he does not, just like my friend's son, he is going to get put out of the house. Likewise when *you* are faced with the same choice, "Do I obey God, or do I not obey God," and if you want to move forward with Him, apply the Nike principle and "just do it."

"This is My covenant which you shall keep...." God is being very clear here. It is no longer about God blessing and Abraham receiving. God wants something from Abraham. He is about to ask Abraham to prepare for something much greater in the future. Please understand this about God: it is not about selfish personal gain. For God, it never is. God needs Abraham to participate in this covenant, and participate willingly, because once again He has a "forever" plan in mind that is for your benefit, not necessarily His. His method to accomplish this only proves how awesome, powerful, and full of wisdom the Lord Almighty is.

Say What?

"Every male child among you shall be circumcised; and you shall be circumcised in the flesh of your foreskins, and it shall be a sign of the covenant between Me and you. He who is eight days old among you shall be circumcised, every male child in your generations, he who is

born in your house or bought for money must be circumcised, and My
covenant shall be in your flesh for an everlasting covenant."
—Genesis 17: 9-14

If you are a guy, I don't think I need to tell you that this is a pretty radical request on the part of God. If you are a woman, I still don't need to tell you how radical this is. Yet Abraham was willing to obey this command and he was willing to require everyone associated with him to comply. He made it the culture of his household.

Don't think for a minute that God takes this command lightly. He was serious about His covenant then and, although you may not realize it, He is still serious about His covenant today. To illustrate this, let's examine the following incident in the life of Moses. Then we will return to our examination of how this all applies to Abraham and the rest of his descendants – including Moses and, by the way, to us as well.

"Now the Lord said to Moses in Midian, 'Go, return to Egypt; for all the men who sought your life are dead.' Then Moses took his wife and his sons and set them on a donkey, and he returned to the land of Egypt. And Moses took the rod of God in his hand... And it came to pass on the way, at the encampment, that the Lord met him and sought to kill him. Then Zipporah took a sharp stone and cut off the foreskin of her son and cast it at Moses' feet, and said, 'Surely you are a husband of blood to me!' So He (God) let him go. Then she said, 'You are a husband of blood!—because of the circumcision.'"
—Exodus 4: 19-20 & 24-26

Wow! God was about to kill Moses over his failure to honor the covenant and circumcise his son. When I read this account, I can't help but wonder what it was, what sort of horror Zipporah encountered, to cause her to grab the first sharp stone she was able to find, cut off the foreskin of her son and throw it at Moses' feet. You can actually hear the terror in her voice as you read of this encounter with an angry God.

I believe the author of the Book of Hebrews may have had a similar revelation, which caused him to pen the following:

> *"**For if we sin willfully** after we have received the knowledge of the truth, there no longer remains a sacrifice for sins, but a certain fearful expectation of judgment, and fiery indignation that will devour the adversaries.* (Which by the way, are all those who choose to rebel against God.) *Anyone who has rejected Moses' law dies without mercy on the testimony of two or three witnesses. Of how much worse punishment, do you suppose, will be thought worthy who has trampled the Son of God underfoot, counted **the blood of the covenant** by which he was sanctified **a common thing**, and insulted the Spirit of grace? For we know Him who said, 'Vengeance is Mine, I will repay,' says the Lord. And again, 'The Lord will judge His people.' **It is a fearful thing to fall into the hands of the living God."***
> **—Hebrews 10: 26-31**

Keep that in mind while we explore the Moses situation. The key word in this Scripture is the word "willfully." Moses knew of the covenant culture of God. I have no doubt that his mother passed this along to him. It was part of his identity as a Hebrew, which we know was imparted to Moses, being that this is what caused him to kill the Egyptian guard forty years prior to this encounter.

Certainly Moses himself was circumcised, yet he failed to obey the Lord in regard to his own family. He willfully left his child with a foreskin. God was not acting randomly in this incident. This blatant omission would have destroyed his credibility amongst his brethren. It was imperative for Moses to be part of the Hebrew culture. He would have never been taken seriously as a Hebrew and thus would have been unable to perform his duty as deliverer of the Israelites. His child should have been circumcised on the eighth day after birth and he knew it.

Once again we see the recurring problem of allowing the wife to supplant the authority of the husband. Look at Zipporah's reaction. She immediately circumcises the child. How did she know to do this? I can just imagine the contentions that must have arisen over this issue. I can envision the conversation, "Zipporah, may I speak with you for a moment?" Remember, Moses was quite humble. I'm sure he was a gentleman.

"The God of my father's requires that we cut off the foreskin of our male children on their eighth day of life. Now I brought this knife because if we don't, God's going to be real angry."

Zipporah then loses her mind. With her finger waving and her head swerving from side to side she proclaims, "You want to do what, to what? Oh, hell no! There is no *way* you are going to harm and disfigure my child in any way, shape or form, and I don't care how angry *your* God gets."

"But Zipporah, you don't understand...."

"Moses, drop the subject. That will happen over my dead body." She did not realize the dead body would have been her husband's. Finally, after hours of quarreling, Moses relents.

I am pretty certain that Moses explained the covenant of circumcision to Zipporah as well because (1) she knew exactly what to do, and (2) Zipporah replies with, *"Surely you are a husband of blood to me—because of the circumcision."*

Each time a child was circumcised, their blood was spilled. Just as Jesus' blood was spilled, the circumcision is a foreshadowing of what was to come. The lack of foreskin, the disfigurement if you will, was a continual reminder of the blood covenant between God and man. In addition, this area of the body symbolizes life through reproduction.

It is Christ who gives us life through the New Covenant. Each person trusting in it is reborn, that is, reproduced into the Kingdom of Heaven. Moses, by heeding the voice of His wife and not circumcising his children, *willfully* failed to instill both God's covenant and His culture into the lives of his children, and it nearly cost him his life.

It is a fearful thing to fall into the hands of the living God. What did Zipporah see that day? I made a mind-blowing discovery while researching this Scripture before a youth meeting that I was conducting. I was intending to preach about the fear of God when I decided to look up the original Greek word translated into English as "fearful." Do you know what it is? It is the Greek word "Omega." That's right, Omega, as in Alpha and Omega.

What is really interesting is the usage of the word. We all know that Alpha is the first letter of the Greek alphabet and Omega is the last. God refers to Himself as both the Alpha and Omega. The significance of using the word Omega in this instance is its expressed implication of finality. The word is used in the Scripture to denote the end. The final end, as in, it's over. The Scripture more accurately translated says, *it is Omega to fall into the hands of the living God,* or, *it is final to fall into the hands of the living God.* The Scripture denotes not just fear, but judgment. The *final* judgment! I hope you realize that God is not playing games with you.

So what did Zipporah see that day? She saw her husband falling into the hands of the living God. She saw her husband falling into the hands of the Omega. She saw Moses' life coming to its final end.

We always want to know God as the Alpha. It feels good to know Him as the beginning. If Jesus Christ is your Lord and Savior, you will know Him as the Alpha forever. For those who rebel, however, and who choose to disobey, He is the Omega. The end! He is the final judgment for all of eternity.

So once again I ask, "What did Zipporah see?" She saw her husband falling into judgment. It so terrified her that she took the foreskin of her son and threw it at the feet of Moses for both he and the Lord to see. The blood had been spilled. The covenant had been ratified and, because God is a merciful God, He relented. Most people never realize that it is God's culture to relent. We are simply too busy listening to the wrong voices, many of which have no real understanding of who He is. How many times has He relented in our lives? Perhaps we will never know until we meet Him face to face.

Do you want to experience this same mercy from God? Circumcise the foreskin of your heart. Enter into covenant with God by accepting the blood of Christ, which has been spilled for you. God's guarantee is to relent. He will forgive your sin and you will escape judgment. We saw this very example on Moses' journey back to Egypt. Without Christ, you are as close to experiencing the judgment of God as Moses was. *"It is a fearful thing to fall into the hands of the living God."* With that settled, let's return to our journey with Abraham. We still have much to learn.

— CHAPTER 5 —

From Promise to Covenant

Three in One

We are about to be blessed with an interesting yet controversial revelation. Abraham is about to have a heavenly visitation. The question is, who are these visitors and what is their purpose? To find out, let's return to Scripture and discover this amazing and unique appearance of the Lord God Almighty. Abraham is about to fully immerse himself into God culture. He is going to experience firsthand the immeasurable blessings contained in the kingdom of God. If you are willing to enter the Lord's gates, you will find that this still holds true today, some five thousand years later.

> *"Then the Lord appeared to Abraham by the terebinth trees of Mamre, as he was sitting in the tent door in the heat of the day. So he lifted*

his eyes and looked, and behold, three men were standing by him; and when he saw them he ran from the tent door to meet them, and bowed himself to the ground, and said, 'Lord if I have found favor in your sight, do not pass on by your servant...'

Then they said to him, 'Where is Sarah your wife?' So he said, 'Here, in the tent.' And He said, 'I will certainly return to you according to the time of life, and behold, Sarah your wife shall have a son.' (Sarah was listening in the tent door, which was behind him.) *Now Abraham and Sarah were old, well advanced in age, and Sarah had passed the age of childbearing. Therefore, Sarah laughed **within herself**, saying, 'After I have grown old, shall I have pleasure, my lord being old also?'*

And the Lord said to Abraham, 'Why did Sarah laugh, saying, 'Shall I surely bear a child, since I am old?' Is anything too hard for the Lord? At the appointed time I will return to you, according to the time of life, and Sarah shall have a son.' But Sarah denied it, saying, 'I did not laugh,' for she was afraid. And He said, 'No, but you did laugh.'"

—Genesis 18: 1-3 & 9-15

The controversy regarding this incident is in regard to the following question: Who are these visitors? There are two theories. Theory number one is that they were angels. Theory number two is that due to its triune nature, three "men," this was a revelation of God Almighty. Believe it or not, I believe each theory has a measure of validity but neither is completely correct. Here is why.

First, the Scripture says that *the Lord* appeared to Abraham. The Hebrew word translated as "Lord" is Yehovah. This is only used as a reference to the Almighty God of Israel. It is actually His name. Abraham may or may not have immediately recognized Him as God because Abraham addressed Him as Adonai. Adonai is actually a Hebrew word that means "governor," but was often used to address the Lord Almighty, who governs all things.

By the way, "Adonai" is a plural word used to address God in many other portions of Scripture, but has been translated into English using the singular form of "God" or "Lord." This is simply a result of the limitation of the English language's ability to accurately describe the nature of God. The Hebrew form is clear that the inert nature of God is that of plurality, Father, Son, and Holy Spirit, united together as one. Just as a man's triune nature of spirit, soul, and body does not make each one of us three different people, God's triune nature is of oneness as well. It is therefore no coincidence that Abraham encounters *three* men.

I also noticed that the translators of the New King James version of the Bible were inconsistent in their usage of the capitalization of the pronoun "He." Sometimes they capitalized it, and sometimes they did not. This means that they were either confused, or what I feel is more accurate is that we have both the Divine and an accompaniment of angels participating in this rendezvous.

Secondly, when Abraham met up with his visitors, he bowed himself to the ground. On every occasion throughout the Scriptures where a man bows himself before any representative of God, the messenger commands the man to get up. *"...and I fell at his feet to worship him. But he said to me, 'See that you do not do that! I am your fellow servant and of your brethren who have the testimony of Jesus. Worship God! ... "* (Revelation 19: 10) We do not see this here. We see Abraham being permitted to bow before Him. Therefore, God must have been present.

Thirdly, when Sarah laughed within herself, the visitor, or more accurately, one of the visitors, immediately discerned it. The last time I checked, it was God and God alone who is omniscient. Angels do not read thoughts. They simply carry out a command of God. Yet the Almighty had the ability to hear Sarah laugh *within herself,* she did not laugh out loud.

Finally, let's examine the following Scripture. *"Now the two angels came to Sodom in the evening... "* (Genesis 19: 1) If you are paying attention, you will notice one inconsistency. There were two angels that showed up in Sodom, but Abraham had three visitors. Yet the Word clearly states that two of them were angels. This means that either the Word is flawed, or the three visitors were clearly not the same beings. Take note of how Abraham's meeting concludes.

> *"Then the men rose from there and looked toward Sodom, and Abraham went with them to send them on the way... And the Lord said, 'Because the outcry against Sodom and Gomorrah is great... I will go down now to see... Then the men turned away from there and went toward Sodom, but Abraham stood still before the Lord."* (Genesis 18: 16, 20, and 22) *"Now the two angels came to Sodom in the evening..."*
>
> **—Genesis 19: 1**

Clearly it was God and two angels that showed up that day. We see two "men" leaving and God staying behind with Abraham "standing still before" Him. Standing still means that they were not in motion and not heading down to Sodom with the other two angels. You do realize that God does not have to physically travel to Sodom to see what is going on, right? He stayed put with Abraham and sent the angels to rescue Lot. We then see two angels show up in Sodom to deliver the news of what just took place to Lot.

Interestingly enough, the Hebrew word translated above as "men" is the Hebrew word "enowah" which is pronounced "en-oaeh". It is used to describe a mortal being, or a man, a human if you will, and I have no doubt whatsoever that they appeared in the likeness of mortal men. So did Jesus.

However, one of the not so common uses of the word enowah is "servant." So let's put two and two together. Oftentimes God requires us to think and analyze. What are angels? Let's allow the Scripture to answer that question. *"Are they not all ministering spirits sent forth to minister for those who will inherit salvation?"* (Hebrews 1:14)

If we pick this scripture apart even further, after discovering that angels are *all* ministering spirits sent to minister to those who will inherit salvation, we must ask ourselves the following question, "What does the word "minister" mean?" Quite simply it means "to serve." That means angels are "enowah." They are servants.

Let's go even further. Who are angels sent forth to serve, who do they minister to? Scripture has two answers: God and man. They serve God and He sends them forth to serve those who will inherit salvation.

Why is God Almighty revealing Himself and entering into covenant with Abraham? The answer to that question and the purpose of God's covenant with mankind is to bring forth salvation. It is really that simple. Therefore, it is perfectly logical and consistent with the Word of God that these visitors were God Almighty, accompanied by His holy angels whose purpose was to minister or serve the heirs of salvation; namely, Abraham, Sarah, and his nephew Lot and his family.

That is exactly what we see them accomplish just before the Lord annihilates Sodom and Gomorrah. God reveals the plan to His covenant partner and the "enowah" go before God to pull several heirs of salvation, Lot and his family, out of the judgment which could only result in their imminent demise.

There was a two-fold purpose for *this* visit. *Everything* God does has purpose. Therefore, let's think about why God did not just destroy Sodom and Gomorrah. Why did He feel obligated to inform Abraham? After all, God is God and He can do whatever he pleases.

I believe the answer is as follows. First, the Lord needed to confirm to Abraham that He still had every intention of fulfilling His promise of blessing Abraham with a son, and that He certainly still possessed the power to do so. Second, He still intends to uphold His end of the covenant and He is completely willing to share everything that He is doing with Abraham. He is being a cultural example to Abraham of how to behave in a covenant relationship.

"And the Lord said, 'Shall I hide from Abraham what I am doing, since Abraham shall surely become a great and mighty nation, and all the families of the earth shall be blessed in him? For I have known him…" (Genesis 18: 17-19) As always, God is being selfless.

Human Life Value

Have you ever considered why self-indulgence is such a horrendous act of rebellion against God? The Lord God, who has both the authority and the right to be more self-indulgent than any being in the universe, always acts in the best interest of mankind. His nature and His culture is contrary to the self-indulgence we have experienced within mankind since the beginning of time.

Satan's nature and his culture is the exact opposite of God's. *The thief does not come except to steal, kill, and destroy.* That is the epitome of self-indulgence. **God, however, values your life—even above His own!** *"God demonstrates His own love toward us, for when we were still sinners Christ died for us."* (Romans 5:8)

Get a revelation of that. While you were still in absolute rebellion against God, He valued your life in favor of His own and died for you on the cross at Calvary. God died...for you. Consider that for a moment and then move on to the next paragraph.

Becoming a Man

At this point, Abraham begins to catch this revelation and we begin to see a shift in his disposition. Since he is moving past the "promise" stage in his relationship with God, he no longer possesses the "all about me" frame of mind. As a result, we begin to see God granting Abraham his covenant rights, which include that God will not hide his plans from him. Since God does not favor one person above another (Acts 10:34), this also holds true for you when you enter into covenant with Him as well. Abraham now has the privilege of petitioning the Almighty.

> *"And Abraham came near and said, 'Would You also destroy the righteous with the wicked? Suppose there were fifty righteous within the city; would You also destroy the place and not spare it for the fifty righteous that were in it? Far be it from You do to such a thing as this, to slay the righteous with the wicked, so that the righteous*

*should be as the wicked; far be it from You! Shall not the Judge of
all the earth do right?*

*So the Lord said, 'If I find in Sodom fifty righteous within the
city, then I will spare all the city for their sakes.'*

*Then Abraham answered and said, 'Indeed now, I who am but
dust and ashes **have taken it upon myself** to speak to the Lord;
suppose there were five less than fifty…forty…thirty…twenty…ten…
And He said, 'I will not destroy it for the sake of ten.'"*
—Genesis 18: 23-33)

The truth is that God found only four righteous within the
city of Sodom. They were Lot, his wife, and his two daughters,
and He removed them from the path of judgment. The rest of the
"Sodomites" were destroyed with the city. The point is, God was
willing not only to listen to Abraham, but to relent at his request.
We see this same character of God throughout the life of Moses and
even within the story of Jonah.

Interestingly enough, just like He did with Moses throughout
his life, God is not finished with Abraham yet either. Until we have
breathed our last breath, there is always something bigger and more
challenging for us when we walk with Him. We see this confirmed
all throughout the Word of God. The longer and more intimate I
become with God, the more I realize that He is never finished with
us. To be honest with you, I find this to be exciting. It gives us reason
to live. It gives us purpose. I am honored that God is still willing to
use me. Yes, the challenges are greater, but so are the rewards.

*"We are always on the anvil; by trials
God is shaping us for higher things"*
—Henry Ward Beecher

If you don't realize this, you can live your entire life in remorse
and despair because you may never understand the purpose of the

trials you are experiencing. This is simply not God's culture. He does not find pleasure in your misery. Will you make mistakes? Of course you will, but God will always give you a second chance, and a third, and a fourth, and as many as you need to get it right, as long as your heart remains with Him. Don't ever believe that you have missed your chance and God's call. I don't care how old you are. Unlike humanity, God's talent never diminishes. *"For the gifts and the calling of God are irrevocable."* (Romans 11: 29) Irrevocable means it cannot ever be rescinded.

If you are still breathing, God can still use you. In God culture, you are never too young and never too old. He has a purpose for you that leads you all the way up to your last breath. I have actually seen with my own eyes the manifestation of God come through a woman on her deathbed. The lives of *every* person in that room were forever changed, including mine.

As she was slipping into eternity, she was still coherent enough to describe what she was experiencing. Her fear was transformed into utter bliss as she saw the room filling with the Holy Angels of the Lord. As she breathed her last breath, she described being carried away by the Lord Jesus Himself…and then she quite simply left her body en route to her eternal home. We discovered the authenticity of God in greater depth through death than we had in life. To me, that makes perfect sense since the entire plan of redemption results in your being escorted into eternity with Him.

Fulfilling the Promise

Let's look at another "now vs. forever" situation. In my opinion this one contains the *second* most obedient act I can recall in the Bible. To prepare for this, however, let's first witness the miraculous.

*"And the Lord visited Sarah **as He said**, and the Lord did for Sarah **as He had spoken**. For Sarah conceived and bore Abraham a son in his old age, **at the set time** of which God had spoken to him. And*

Abraham called the name of his son who was born to him—whom
Sarah bore to him—Isaac."
—Genesis 21: 1-3

There are a couple of things that are made very clear in these
verses of Scripture. Isaac was born "at the set time." Not Abraham's
set time; God's set time. God is always in control, even when you
do not realize it.

God also makes it perfectly clear that Isaac is to receive the
promise. Isaac is the one born into and as a result of the covenant.
Why is this important? Let's step back to Genesis 17 for a moment
to answer this question. God has just revealed to Abraham that
Isaac will be born in exactly one year. Abraham finds this to be so
outlandish that he, like Sarah, actually falls to the ground laughing.

"'...Shall a child be born to a man who is one hundred years old? And
shall Sarah, who is ninety years old, bear a child?' And Abraham said
to God, 'Oh, that Ishmael might live before you!'"
—Genesis 17: 17-18

In essence, Abraham said to God, "Lord, we are old. There is no
way we can have children. Establish your covenant through Ishmael."
At this point, Abraham is having a difficult time understanding the
power of God. I do not think he has a clear grasp of what God is
going to accomplish through him. However, God knows what he is
about to do; and He replies as follows. Now pay attention to this
because it is infinitely important, literally.

"Then God said: 'No, Sarah your wife shall bear a son, and you shall
call his name Isaac; I will establish My covenant with him for an
everlasting covenant, and with his descendants after him. And
as for Ishmael I have heard you. Behold, I have blessed him, and
have made him fruitful, and will multiply him exceedingly. But My

covenant I will establish with Isaac, whom Sarah shall bear to you at this set time next year."
—Genesis 17: 19-21

If you are unaware of theological history, I must tell you that this is not only one of the most relevant Scriptures in the Bible, but aside from the revelation of Jesus Christ, it is perhaps *the* most important. In fact, as I will illustrate to you shortly, it *is* a revelation of Jesus Christ, thus equating it in relevance.

God is never ambiguous and He is making something very clear. His covenant is through Isaac, not Ishmael. In fact, this culture of covenant is so vital that it is to be passed down from generation to generation for the remainder of time. That is what "everlasting" means.

If you have any knowledge of the Q'ran, you will note that it claims Ishmael to be the son of promise, not Isaac. God makes perfectly clear in the Book of Genesis that the opposite is true. You may be thinking this is their word against ours. The truth is that there are three major religions in the world. They are, listed in chronological order of their appearance: Judaism, Christianity, and Islam. All three have based their theological doctrine upon the Law of Moses and all three of these believe the patriarch Abraham is their origin and that Abraham offered up a son.

However, Islam splits with the others in the account of the offering. Both Judaism and Christianity believe it was Isaac. Only Islam purports the offering to have been that of Ishmael. However, based upon the Law of Moses, which is the basis of all three religions, it requires a minimum of two witnesses to establish any legal matter. (Deuteronomy 17: 6) Therefore, since Judaism and Christianity agree regarding this matter and Islam stands alone, the Islamic account is condemned as false according to this law, which *is* the basis of Islam.

Therefore, I must conclude that Islam leads one into deception based upon its own law. Take note that I did not condemn it as a false religion. As a religion, it is as valid as any religion on the planet. One must deduce, however, that it is devoid of any and all salvation, being that the foundations of its principles are in direct contradiction to God's Law, which, as we will see later, leads one *to* and not *away* from Christ.

As such, according to the Law of Moses, the covenant was clearly established in Isaac, not Ishmael. Remember, God operates from the standpoint of foresight. He is ever present in the past, present and the future. He knew Islam would rise up and what their claim would be. Therefore, He addressed the issue. The preservation of the true covenant is why the Lord went through such great pains to emphasize who the true sacrificial "lamb" was.

In addition, let's rely on some basic human logic. I listed the religions in chronological order for a purpose. Let's say that I was to publish a story today and, one year later, the same story was to be published by a different author, but that author changed the storyline of the book. Who would be responsible for changing the story: author one or author two? Obviously it had to be author two who changed the story, since he or she published the same story at a later date based on the timeline of events.

The same holds true in regard to "religion." The earliest accounts of the Epistles were written somewhere between seventy and one hundred years after Christ lived; the Gospels even earlier, even as close as twenty years or so. They are often times first-hand accounts that perfectly match our versions of the Bible today. The Dead Sea scrolls contain the oldest version of the Book of Isaiah known to man. It also perfectly matches our account of Isaiah today contained within the pages of the Bible and the Torah.

However, the Q'ran, written almost six hundred years *after* the death of Jesus Christ, and four hundred-fifty years after the Biblical canon was compiled and authenticated, changes the accounts of several prophets, as well as Jesus Christ's birth. It places several historically confirmed Old Testament prophets along the wrong timeline, matches up their ancestors incorrectly, and changes the Isaac and Ishmael account. Now based upon pure logic alone, who changed the stories?

If we can historically prove that the timeline of events and lineages within the Q'ran are incorrect, and make no mistake, we can, it had to be Mohammed and/or at least one of his scribes, being that he himself was illiterate. That, in and of itself, is problematic to the authenticity of the Q'ran. Mohammed could not read or write, so he could not corroborate what was actually being recorded.

I am sure there are some very astute people who will say, "Well, both Judaism and Islam do not believe that Jesus was the Messiah. That is two witnesses against one. Jesus also must be false and Judaism must be false as well. They too do not agree."

On the surface it may seem like a valid question, but it is an incorrect conclusion. If you have never studied the Word of God, it is quite easy to fall into this deception. The Old Testament, however, is very clear that the Messiah would be born. In fact, the Old Testament actually tells us exactly who that person is, down to the town He would be born in, how He would enter Jerusalem, how, in detail, He would die, the fact that He would be divine, amongst a plethora of additional details. It is even possible to trace the year that he would ride into Jerusalem on a donkey, and yes, it names a donkey (Zechariah 9:9).

Islam purports that the same Biblical account of Zechariah also foresees the rise of the "prophet" Mohammed. They claim that the mention of the camel in Zechariah 14:15 is a reference to a "prophet" rising out of Arabia. Keep in mind that the camel being mentioned, which is allegedly a representative of Islam, and the prophet Mohamed, is in reference to a "day of the Lord" plague, which is a judgment coming upon those who fought against Jerusalem (Zechariah 14:12).

"Behold the day of the Lord is coming... And this shall be the plague with which the Lord will strike all the people who fought against Jerusalem."
—Zechariah 14:1 and 12

I do not believe this interpretation to be accurate. It simply appears to be a reference to animals but not an allegory to in reference to religious groups. If it is, however, keep in mind that Islam has been fighting against Jerusalem since its inception. That most certainly puts them on the wrong side of the law and in the path of judgment.

Also according to Islam, Isaiah 21:7 foretells the rise of Islam and Mohammed. Keep in mind that if this *is* true, and I actually believe it is, the prophecy comes from the Bible and not the Q'ran, thus providing even further evidence of the authenticity and foresight of the true Word of God. The Q'ran has no fulfilled prophecy.

With that said, however, let's go back to verse 6 of Isaiah 21 and see what it actually does reveal. *"For thus has the Lord said to me: Go, set a watchman, let him declare what he sees."* Watchmen were set in place to spot the enemy before they attacked a city or encampment. Keep that "enemy" part in mind. Let's continue on: *"And he saw a chariot with a pair of horsemen, a chariot of donkeys,* **and a chariot of camels,** *and he listened earnestly with great care."*

The symbolism here is clear and is a foretelling of the rise of the three great religions: Judaism being represented by the horsemen, Christianity by the donkeys, and Islam by the chariot of camels. I believe this revelation to be accurate both in its foresight and, as discussed earlier, in its chronological order. However, what no one, especially the followers of Islam, has realized is that verse 8 declares, *"Then he cried, a lion, my Lord!"*

If you believe that the first three accounts are accurate, then you cannot separate or omit verse 8 which declares, *"a Lion!"* This is clearly a revelation of the return of the Messiah, Jesus Christ, who is also known as **The Lion of the Tribe of Judah** who has returned to put a final end to evil.

Let's read the rest of verse 8 and continue with verse 9. Keep in mind as you read this that while Christianity is patiently awaiting the return of the Messiah, Judaism also awaits the appearance of the Messiah and the ushering in of His eternal Kingdom, thus the reference to "standing continually on the watchtower."

"I stand continually on the watchtower in the daytime; I have sat at my post every night. And look, here come a chariot of men with a pair of horsemen. Then he answered and said, 'Babylon is fallen, is fallen! And all the carved images of her gods He has broken to the ground.'"
—Isaiah 21:6-10

This is irrefutably a revelation of the fulfillment of the Lord's covenant with all the major players in place and in the correct chronological order. Once again Islam is in the path of judgment as the prophet declares, "Babylon (which is located in modern day Iraq) is fallen, is fallen." Every false god and religion will be broken to the ground. Only Jesus Christ and His saints will be left standing.

There are actually hundreds of details that Jesus alone could fulfill. So once again, it is two against one. A person's disbelief or even an entire race of people disbelieving does not nullify the truth of God. In actuality, both the Old and New Testaments agree that Jesus Christ of Nazareth is the Messiah.

A careful study of the Book of Romans will explain to you why God blinded the eyes of the Jewish people. Suffice it to say that your salvation was at stake and God needed to pull you into His covenant. The Jews who have rejected Him will believe and accept Him upon His return as the Lion in the above reference reveals. You may not like this, but it is truth. It is part of His covenant and God will never abandon His chosen people.

Also keep in mind that God did exactly what He said He would do for Ishmael. He said He would multiply Ishmael exceedingly. With over one billion Muslims in the world, who are the descendants of Ishmael, I would have to say that God made good on this promise as well.

However, this was a promise, not a covenant. You must understand the difference to comprehend the truth. God even said that Islam, the descendants of Ishmael, would be "wild men." Only wild men would run around the Middle East and the rest of the world blowing themselves up along with a multitude of innocent people. That is against every cultural element that Almighty God has ever implemented. God made good His promise to bless Ishmael and He made good on His promise to bring salvation through the covenant made with Abraham, Isaac, and Jacob.

He also revealed the culture of Ishmael's descendants. The Islamic culture of violence instituted by Mohammed himself has manifested consistently in every country they have inhabited throughout history. God did not hide the truth. He is very open about it, and it is your personal responsibility to seek it. With that in mind, let's now see a detailed illustration of the Messiah revealed in Isaac, and let's watch Abraham give his all to the covenant of God.

Back to the Future

> *"Now it came to pass after these things that God tested Abraham, and said to Him, 'Abraham!' And he said, 'Here I am.' Then He said, 'Take now your son, your only son Isaac, whom you love, and go to the land of Moriah, and offer him there as a burnt offering there on one of the mountains which I tell you.'"*
>
> **—Genesis 22: 1-2**

First and foremost, allow me to preface with an observation. God will *never* ask you to do this! As you will see, God is requiring this of Abraham for a specific purpose that only needs to be fulfilled one time. God does not and will not ever require another human sacrifice. Only once in the history of the universe was there a human sacrifice required, and that was the sacrifice of Jesus Christ of Nazareth to obliterate the sin of all those willing to believe.

It is the only human blood that God ever has, and will, require because it was His own blood. No one else's blood is worthy. Therefore, if God ever asks you to sacrifice one of your children, seek professional help because it is not God who is speaking to you. (Romans 6:10). So with that in mind, you should be asking: "Why is God demanding that Isaac be slain?"

In order to truly comprehend the culture of the Almighty, we must understand the following about His approach to mankind. *"...I am God and there is no other; I am God and there is none like Me; **declaring the end from the beginning,** and from ancient times **things that are not yet done.**"* (Isaiah 46: 9-10) And, *"That which has been is what will be, that which is done is what will be done, and there is nothing new under the sun."* (Ecclesiastes 1:9)

If you want to understand what God will do in the future, you must look to the past. It is the key to understanding any and all prophecy and it is a major element of God culture. His prophetic ability sets Him apart from every other so-called deity man has ever dreamed up, and He loves to show off His ability and share it with us. God does not keep secrets from us. As we will see later, He keeps secrets *for* us. God's culture is to reveal what He is going to do in the future by pointing you to what He has already done in the past.

Therefore, if we want to understand God's perfect plan of redemption, which is available to all mankind today, we must look to the past. We must look to the Old Covenant. To truly understand the New Covenant, you must understand the Old Covenant. The implementation of the Old Covenant, as well as, the beginning of God culture, begins with Abraham.

To begin, let's have a look at the language that God uses with Abraham. He said, *"Abraham, take your son, your **only son, whom you love**, and sacrifice him..."* Let's compare this to what God states in the following Scriptures. *"For God so loved the world that He gave **His only** begotten Son..."* (John 3:16) *"And suddenly a voice came from heaven, saying, 'This is My **beloved** Son, in whom I am well pleased.'"* (Matthew 3:17) *"In this the love of God was manifested toward us, that God has sent His only begotten Son into the world, that we might live through Him. In this is love, not that we loved God, but that He loved us and sent His Son to be the propitiation for our sins."* (1 John 4: 9-11)

Can you see what God is doing in light of what we have just learned? He is making a declaration of the covenant, and His willingness to uphold His end of it. He is declaring the end from the beginning. God will never ask you to do anything that He is not willing to do Himself. When God asked Abraham to sacrifice his son, God was not only willing, but offered up His own Son as well.

This is the difference between God and Allah. It is totally contrary to the ideology of Allah who asks his people to die, to sacrifice their own lives, as well as, the lives of their children, and yet he offers nothing in return, only a scale to weigh your good against your bad. He offers no guarantees and no reassurance.

Not even Mohammed was one hundred percent sure of his own eternal fate. To this day, included in every Muslim daily prayer is a petition for mercy upon the soul of Mohammed. Islam contains no guarantee *and* no covenant. Only YHWH, the only true and living God, offers a guarantee through the New Covenant cut with the body and blood of Jesus Christ, the atoning Lamb of God Who takes away the sin of the world.

Upon further examination, we find that Isaac is a type of Christ. He was a foreshadowing of what was to come. Isaac was a living illustration of God declaring the end from the beginning. As we continue, this will become undeniably clear. As you read on, there will be no doubt that Jesus is the Messiah. Jesus, beyond any shadow of a doubt, is the End that God declared from the beginning.

I'll Be Back

Let's return to our discussion of Abraham. *"So Abraham rose early in the morning and saddled his donkey…"* I must tell you that Abraham is a better man than I am. There was no arguing with God. No reasoning. He just accepted what God told him, saddled up his donkey, and shoved off.

> *"So Abraham rose early in the morning and saddled up his donkey, and took two of his young men with him, and Isaac his son; and he split the wood for the burnt offering, and arose and went to the place which God had told him. Then on the third day* (Three days is not a coincidence here. This is the number of days Jesus spent in the grave prior to His resurrection) *Abraham lifted his eyes and saw the place afar off. And Abraham said to his young men, 'Stay here with the donkey, the lad and I will go yonder and worship, **and we will come back to you.**'"*
> **—Genesis 22: 3-5**

Contained within the Word of God is a principle called the law of double-reference. This law simply means that one Scripture passage can have more than one meaning. We see a beautiful example of the law of double-reference contained within the phrase, *"and we will come back to you."* Abraham was obviously referring to him and Isaac returning after they had accomplished what God had asked of them. This should begin to give you a clue toward Abraham's mindset. However, we also see a beautiful picture of the Messiah contained within this phrase, both in His resurrection and in His second coming at which time He will be accepted by our Hebrew brethren.

Remember, the purpose of this trip was to sacrifice Isaac to God, just like the purpose of Jesus' "trip" to the natural realm was to be a sacrifice for all mankind. After the death and resurrection of Jesus Christ, He ascended into heaven to be seated at the right hand of the Father. At some future point, He will *"come back to"* mankind as Judge and will set up His eternal kingdom.

In Abraham and Isaac, we see the same picture. We see Abraham acting as the Father and sacrificing his only begotten son Isaac, who has taken on the role of Jesus Christ, who later returns to his people following his death and resurrection. While Abraham was referring to a current or very near future event, he was also prophesying about what God was planning to do later. Incredibly, Abraham, Isaac, and God were all declaring the end from the beginning. Remember the story of Joseph that we analyzed and discussed in chapter one? Didn't it follow the same principle?

This brings us to an interesting point that actually allows us a glimpse into Abraham's mind so many years ago. Abraham makes the statement, "...the lad and I will go yonder and worship." Do you know what I find amazing? In the midst of all the stress Abraham was feeling and experiencing—and please do not be fooled; he was "stressed out"—Abraham viewed the sacrifice of his own son as an act of worship to the great Creator of the universe.

Don't forget that God has promised Abraham that his "seed" will be as the stars in the heavens. Remember all the looking up at the sky, and changing his name to the "father of many nations," and all of that faith building "stuff" that God had Abraham do earlier in the story? It worked. Abraham became so fully convinced that God would do what He said He would do, that Abraham was even willing to give God his only son, the son born of a promise and a miracle, of a woman in whom it was physically impossible to have children with.

This can also be viewed as a picture of the virgin birth. Sarah was old and barren and could not have children unless God intervened and provided the seed through an undeniable miracle. Since Mary was a virgin, it was also impossible for her to have children unless God intervened and provided a Seed through an undeniable miracle, which He also did. God always declares the end from the beginning.

He's Alive

That brings us to Abraham's "million dollar" question, which was also his greatest dilemma. How can he possibly become the father of many nations if his only offspring lies dead in the grave? The answer:

*"By faith, Abraham when he was tested, offered up Isaac, and he who had received the promises offered up his **only begotten son,** of whom it was said, 'In Isaac your seed shall be called,' **concluding that God was able to raise him up, even from the dead,** from which he also received him in a figurative sense."* (Hebrews 11: 17-19) Abraham *"did not waver at the promise of God through unbelief, but was strengthened in his faith, giving glory to God, and being fully persuaded that what He had promised He was also able to perform."* (Romans 4:20-21)

Abraham actually set out on the journey that morning believing that God would raise Isaac from the dead. Why not? In Abraham's view, God had done it before. Sarah's womb was dead. Abraham, being one hundred years old, for childbearing purposes, was dead. This is what the above Scripture means when it says, *"...from which he* (Abraham) *also received him* (Isaac) *in a figurative sense."* Abraham figured, "If God can do it once, He can do it again."

Abraham believed God's promise so fully that he went to Mount Moriah completely intending to slay his only son. Abraham was not joking and was not intending to go only halfway. God culture never goes half way. *"So shall My Word be that goes forth from My mouth; it shall not return to Me void, but it shall accomplish what I please, and it shall prosper in the thing for which I sent it."* (Isaiah 55:11)

This was not a show on the part of either God or Abraham. There would be no pat on the back. Abraham brought a knife, firewood, and the rope to bind Isaac with. He had every intention of using it, *knowing* that God was going to have to fulfill His end of the bargain. Abraham was one hundred percent convinced that God's promise was true and that he would be the father of many nations.

That left only one option and there was no plan B. God culture never includes plan B. Plan A works one hundred percent of the time. God is infallible that way. Since God had rejected performing the covenant through Ishmael, His (God's) only option, in Abraham's mind, was to raise Isaac from the dead.

Now that's faith! That is the radical, all the way, extremist kind of fanatical faith I want. Not the selfish kind that only considers what I can receive from God, but the kind that makes me willing to give everything for and to Him. That's God culture. That is what He did for me! He gave me everything. Just imagine what might happen if you could elevate your faith to this level. The blessing would be endless and so would be the fruit of your harvest.

We also see an amazingly clear picture of the Messiah within these Scriptures. We see his sacrifice, death, and resurrection. According to Galatians 3:8, God actually preached the Gospel to Abraham some thirty-five hundred years before the birth of Christ. No wonder he was willing to give Isaac. He believed everything God told him, no matter how outlandish it may have seemed.

Take a moment to ask yourself if you would believe everything God tells you, similar to Abraham, no matter how absurd it may seem. Be honest with yourself. That is a difficult question to answer, no matter where you are with God or how mature you may believe you are.

God Will Provide

Based on what we just learned, let's see what elevated faith really looks like:

"So Abraham took the wood of the burnt offering and laid it on his son; and he took the fire in his hand, and a knife, and the two of them went together. But Isaac spoke to Abraham his father and said, 'My father!' (Notice that Isaac is beginning to become alarmed) *And he said, 'Here I am, my son.' Then he said, 'Look, the fire and the wood, but where is the lamb for a burnt offering?'*

They say a picture is worth a thousand words and what a beautiful picture of the Messiah this is. Just as Jesus carried His own cross to Calvary, Isaac carried the wood of the burnt offering to Mount Moriah in preparation of his own sacrifice. Just as God laid the sin of the world on His own Son through the cross, "the wood" of the burnt offering was laid upon Isaac as well.

"And Abraham said, 'My son, God will provide for Himself the lamb for a burnt offering.' So the two of them went off together."
—Genesis 22:6-8

What a profound statement Abraham makes here. Again we see the law of double-reference at work. Abraham is clearly referring to his current dilemma, while at the same time prophesying of the future Messiah, Jesus Christ of Nazareth.

"Then they came to the place of which God had told him. And Abraham built an altar there and placed the wood in order; and he bound Isaac his son and laid him on the altar, upon the wood. And Abraham stretched out his hand and took the knife to slay his son."
—Genesis 22:9-10

Laying It Down

I would like to discuss something here that we never even consider when we read this story. We always discuss the obedience of Abraham, and yes, Abraham was incredibly obedient in this situation, but what about Isaac? No one ever talks about Isaac. By this time, Abraham must be about one hundred eighteen years old or so. That would make Isaac eighteen years old. Allow me to ask another question. Don't you think an eighteen-year-old, young, strong, healthy, youthful man could overcome a one-hundred-plus-year-old man when push comes to shove?

Isaac *had* to have permitted himself to be bound and laid upon that altar. The obedience of Isaac is at least equal and perhaps even more extraordinary than that of Abraham. It was Isaac's life on the line. I have to tell you, if my father took me on a walk and then informed me that he was going to slay me upon the Lord's altar, you can bet there is going to be a fight—and at this point I'm pretty sure I would come out as the winner.

Once again, we see another example of a Messianic scene played out here. Just as Isaac was *willing* to be sacrificed, so was Jesus. In the Gospel of John, Chapter 10:18, Jesus states, *"No one takes My life from Me, but I lay it down of Myself."* Isaac was willing to do exactly the same thing. He was laying down his life. Would you lay down your life for God?

There are crucial implications here that illustrate to us exactly why God chose Abraham above every other human being walking planet Earth at that time. *"For I have known him, in order that he may **command his children and his household after him,** that **they may keep the way of the Lord,** to do righteousness and justice, that the Lord may bring to Abraham what He has spoken to him."* (Genesis 18:19)

That is one heck of a revelation. God chose Abraham because he knew that Abraham would teach his children and everyone in his "household." He knew that Abraham would demand that his children learn and practice God culture.

If you truly want to live a powerfully blessed life, I would encourage you to do the same. Teach God culture to everyone around you, to your children, regardless of their age, and your friends, family, business partners, you name it. When you are willing to do this, you will truly have moved "from promise to covenant" in your relationship with God.

God says, *"...that the Lord may bring to him what He has spoken."* In other words, because of Abraham's willingness to command, or teach God culture to his children, God was willing to command all of the blessings that He poured into the life of Abraham.

There is another even more important reason why commanding his children was the Lord's main requirement. Please notice that God's prerequisite for choosing a man to cut a covenant with had nothing to do with the man's perfection. Just like you and me, Abraham was far from perfect. As you will soon realize, it is quite obvious that Abraham had to have been teaching Isaac about God's will and His ways. There is no doubt that Isaac was intimate with God culture. Isaac had to have had a personal relationship with God. There is no other way he would have been willing to be bound and killed. As a result, God deemed *Abraham* righteous, which means, right with God, in the eyes of God. He had successfully passed God culture to Isaac.

What do you think Abraham and Isaac's conversation sounded like? It must have been something like:

"Isaac, lay down on the altar."

"Uh… What…why?"

"Isaac, get down on the altar! Has God ever let us down before? I know you are scared. I am too. But I also know that God is going to raise you from the dead."

"C'mon, Dad, quit joking around."

"Isaac, look at all that God has done, all that you have seen. I have been teaching you about His greatness and His mercy your whole life. You have even experienced Him yourself. Now He told me He will raise you from the dead."

"Are you sure, Dad?"

"Yes, I'm sure. I love you, Son. You are all I have. You mean everything to me. I would never do anything to harm you. The only one greater is God and He never breaks His promises. You will live again and we will walk down that hill, back to our friends, get back on that donkey, and you will go home with me. Now lay down…"

Bringing the Messiah into the world required more than just a covenant with Abraham. It required Isaac, the sacrifice, to be brought into covenant with God as well. In order for Isaac to partake of this covenant, it was a requirement that Abraham teach him of God's love, mercy, grace, and method of operation—His culture if you will.

It is not that Abraham was an extraordinary man in a worldly sense. He was as ordinary as you and me, but he was always willing to learn. He was undoubtedly an extraordinary teacher and leader of his children and his entire household. That is a quality that God can always work with and one that we can all possess, but it requires the laying down of one's life. It requires you to place God's will above your own.

Avail-ability

Do you realize that you have this same ability available to you, and perhaps, no, without a doubt, an even greater ability? You just need to avail yourself to God. You have the ability because when you enter into covenant with God, it is not your ability, it is His ability and He fills you with His Holy Spirit in order to bring it to pass. You simply need to become available and receive Him.

Your power is not in your ability; it is in your availability. The Holy Spirit of God, who will guide you into all truth (John 16:13), resides within you. You can be as extraordinary as Abraham. Just like him, it has nothing to do with your *ability*, but everything to do with your *availability*! If you are willing, God is able.

Ratification

To conclude this discussion, let's return to Scripture:

> *"But the Angel of the Lord called to him from heaven* (Notice where this call came from. Abraham and Isaac's radical obedience resulted in a call directly from heaven.) *and said, 'Abraham, Abraham!' So he said, 'Here I am.' And He said, 'Do not lay a hand on the lad, or do anything to him; for now I know that you fear God, since you have not withheld your son, your only son, from Me.'"*
> **—Genesis 22:11-12**

I believe that Abraham's raising of the dagger and his every intention of thrusting it through his son is the exact point that mankind was redeemed. Abraham fulfilled the covenant. When Abraham said yes by his actions, not by his words, God also said yes. Now that God knew that Abraham was willing to uphold his end of the covenant by giving Him his son, God also became willing to give His Son.

Do you remember a bit earlier when we discussed the concept of, "If you, then I"? God culture always requires you to step out in faith, to believe His Word and His promises, and make the first move. This is what causes your Covenant Father to move. This is exactly what Abraham did, and it resulted in God's willingness to uphold His end of the covenant and give the Lord Jesus Christ to us.

A Method to His Madness

Our work is not quite finished yet. God did not leave us hanging. He now reveals how He will redeem us. He shows us an important detail that is intended for you to recognize. *"Then Abraham lifted his eyes and looked, and there behind him was a ram caught in a thicket by its horns. So Abraham went and took the ram, and offered it up for a burnt offering **instead of his son.**"* (Genesis 22:13)

The substitution of the ram for Isaac quite obviously reveals the plan of redemption through the death of Jesus Christ. God substituted Christ for you and added the preceding detail of the ram caught in the thicket to be sure there is no chance of mistaken identity. A thicket is a dense development of underbrush, usually containing a growth of thorny bushes. Abraham looks up and finds a ram with its *head* caught in the thicket.

In the crucifixion of Christ, it is the Messiah's head that is caught in the thicket of a twisted crown of thorns. Jesus Christ *is* the Messiah and the fulfillment of the covenant. Jesus Christ is the beginning, middle, and the end of God culture.

Watch Your Mouth

*"Then the Angel of the Lord called to Abraham a second time out of heaven, and said, '**By Myself I have sworn**, says the Lord, because you have done this thing, and not withheld your son, **your only son**—blessing I will bless you, and multiplying I will multiply you… and your descendants **shall possess the gates of their enemies.** In your seed, **all** the nations of the earth shall be blessed, because you have obeyed My voice.'"*

—Genesis 22: 15-18

Notice that God, identified here as the Angel of the Lord, which many theologians have identified as the pre-incarnate Christ, never quite finishes His sentence when He states, *"...your only son..."* in the above Scripture. It is as if He simply did not finish His thought. I believe this pause is a result of the fact that Jesus' time had not yet come. God never has an unfinished thought. He never leaves anything incomplete—and that includes you.

God knew and revealed His intention. The thought was finished, but since everything God says comes to pass, He simply could not yet say it. Had He done so, Jesus would have manifested in the flesh right on the spot. When God said, "Let there be light," there was light. When God said, "Let there be stars," there were stars. When God said, "Let there be waters," there was water. Likewise, when God said, "Let Us make man," man was made. Had God completed that sentence and said, "Since you have given your son, I will give you Mine," someone would have immediately become pregnant! His purpose is clear, but it simply was not the appointed time to say it.

The Son of Man

In Jesus Christ we see the completion of the covenant. His blood being spilled was the culmination of the blood covenant made with Abraham. In contract law, there is a concept called "consideration." It means that a contract is not valid until some form of consideration, or payment, has changed hands in whatever the agreed upon form is. Jesus' blood is the consideration that ratified the New Covenant. Jesus' blood being spilled was a substitute for our blood being spilled. It is the price of sin.

Physical death separated Jesus from the Life of Jehovah, thus resulting in spiritual death. Spiritual death is the eternal separation from God the Father. That is always the judgment of sin. The penalty for this crime is hell, where you will be disconnected from the resurrection Life of God forever.

Therefore, like an ugly tattoo, you must have it removed. You cannot scratch it off yourself. Without the proper technology, a tattoo is permanent and so is your sin without Jesus Christ. The resurrection of Jesus Christ has reconnected Him to the Father. When you become one with Jesus, you become one with the Father. The result is the blotting out of sin and the resurrection of your soul. You *will* die in the flesh, but you no longer have to die in spirit.

Since "*The wages of sin is death,*" (Romans 6:23) and "*All have sinned and fall short of the glory of God,*" (Romans 3:23) we all need a Savior. Sin is man's culture. As you are aware, however, none of us possess the proper wage to redeem ourselves from sin. It requires perfection. The Savior had to be spotless and without sin. He had to be perfect. Since no man could measure up, only God Himself would suffice. Only God is perfect. Nothing and no one else could have been an equal or better sacrifice than the first Adam, the man created by God without sin.

The blood of a bull or goat is insufficient (Hebrew 9:13). It does not cost enough. It does not have enough value. Therefore, it could only temporarily "atone" for our sin, which means "to cover it up," but it could never blot out or remove our sin. Only the "Son of Man," as Jesus referred to Himself, could pay the covenant price. Only Jesus could ever possess the proper wage.

"Son of Man," is a translation of the Hebrew phrase, "Bin Adam." It means the "second Adam." The characteristic of being sinless made Jesus equal to the first Adam, who, although created sinless, caused sin and death to pollute mankind. In truth, Jesus is supremely greater than Adam, as He and the Father are one. He is God. Therefore, only the sinless Jesus is worthy to complete the covenant and replace death with life eternal. As Adam brought sin and death into the world, so Jesus brought life and redemption. Without Jesus' life being substituted for ours, we would all be condemned to death through sin, which leads to a life of eternal separation from the one and only living God. That would mean each of us would have to die spiritually. That is the very definition of hell.

That, however, is unacceptable to God. By His giving of free will to us, and His unwillingness to compromise it, death became the only means of redemption. Only death can separate man from His sin. You must die in spirit to be resurrected to life. That is what it means to be born again.

In the first birth, you are separated from your mother's womb. In the rebirth, you are separated from your sin. Both result in life. The former birth thrusts you into life in the natural. The latter reaps life eternal.

It is utterly amazing how God set this plan in motion. In everything He has accomplished, He has not violated a single one of His laws. He did not make one mistake. Not even in giving us free will. *Every jot and tittle* has been fulfilled. (Matthew 5:18)

Think about this for a moment. Free will is the one attribute God has given us that we continually ask Him to violate every time we make a mistake. We subsequently cry out for Him to fix what we have done. We continually want Him to suspend the law of sowing and reaping. Not only do we ask Him to suspend it, we act as if our mistakes are His fault.

We will deal with this more later but suffice it to say that the more I learn of His love for mankind, and the more I learn about God culture, Christ is without a doubt the best way for God to have redeemed us. I cannot say it was the only way. I am not all knowing. Only God is. It is certainly the only way I can comprehend it, but God is so full of wisdom that there may have been infinite ways for Him to accomplish His will for redemption. I am fully confident that He weighed all of His options before choosing. In knowing God's character, which is Love, and while continually learning His culture, it seems that this is, without a doubt, the best, and, believe it or not, the least painful way of rescuing us.

No Denying Him

If you happen to be reading this book and you are Muslim, or if you would like to be a witness to your Muslim friends, I have a revelation for you. I understand that Muslims believe Ishmael was the son of promise and not Isaac. This contradiction leads me to ask what I consider to be a logical question. If it was Ishmael on the altar, what would have happened to Islam if God went through with the sacrifice?

The answer is that Ishmael would have been killed and Islam would never have existed. The religion of Islam came into being during the life of Mohammed. I know Muslims like to claim that Abraham was Muslim, but how is that possible when history confirms that Islam was born in the year 600 A.D.? In truth, Mohammed would have never been born, since his forefathers would have been eliminated from history. Without Mohammed, there is no Islam.

Even with that in mind, the point is: does Ishmael on the altar change the Messianic prophecy? Remember, God always declares the end from the beginning. By God relenting, He, in essence, raised Ishmael from the dead, in a figurative sense. Just as I discussed earlier with Isaac, God was showing you the New Covenant. The sacrifice *remains* a picture of the Messiah. God was declaring that Jesus Christ, crucified and raised from the dead, is the Savior of mankind, regardless of religion.

Through the obedience of both Abraham and whoever you believe the sacrifice to be, the Savior of mankind is Jesus Christ and not Islam's scale that weighs your good deeds against the bad. Ishmael in place of Isaac does not change the plan of redemption, and it does not change the identity of Jesus Christ.

Consider all of the details and parallels between the sacrifice and Christ. You cannot escape this truth. Carefully consider the fact that you may be basing your eternity on a scale that cannot tip in your favor. Therefore, why not consider placing your eternal "bet" on a guarantee based upon a *covenant* with God that He will not break? I encourage you to choose Christ. Choose God culture. He is *"the way, the truth, and the life. No one comes to the Father except through Him."* (John 14:6) Covenant is the reason why. Covenant *is* God culture.

Made in God's Image

I have often heard the question asked, "Why did God have to come as a man?" Without picking on any one particular religion, Muslims have often proclaimed to me that God would never lower Himself to become a man. Don't you see? By making this statement, you are actually placing your own limitation upon the wisdom of an all knowing and all-powerful God.

Whenever I have a theological discussion with one of my Muslim brothers or sisters, and I have had many, the concept of an "all knowing" and "all-powerful" God always comes up. These phrases are repeated all over the Q'ran as well. In Christianity, we use the terms "omniscient" and "omnipotent" to describe these same concepts. It is certainly one of the great truths of the universe. God is, without a doubt, all knowing and all-powerful. That leads me to believe the following:

The Word of God says that He *"knew us in Christ before the foundation of the world."* (Ephesians 1:4) It also says the *"Lamb of God was slain from the foundation of the world."* (Revelation 13:8) This means that God knew each and every one of us, even before the beginning of time as we know it.

He also not only knew exactly what He was going to do to redeem mankind, and He actually set it into motion before He even created the heavens and the earth. As amazing as this is, wouldn't you agree that it is absolutely consistent with an all knowing and all-powerful God? Does it not declare the end from the beginning? Wouldn't you expect that to be a part of God's culture?

Since God already knew exactly what was going to happen to mankind, and how He would rectify the problem before it even occurred, doesn't it make sense for God to have solved the problem from the beginning, and in the simplest manner available? Salespeople call it "eliminating the objection". God calls it, as we discussed earlier, "declaring the end from the beginning." This means that you simply answer the question before it arises. In God creating man in His own image, this is exactly what He did. He solved the problem before it arose. Note the following sequence of events:

God creates the heavens and the earth. He creates man. Man lives in paradise. Man commits sin and brings death and evil into the world. Man is separated from God. Sin spreads to all of mankind. Every man born into sin is born separated from his Creator. Mankind grows in number and sin. Jesus, who is God incarnate, enters the natural realm of mankind through the spiritual gateway of Mary's womb. Jesus spills His blood and dies with your sin being placed upon Him. Jesus takes that sin to a separate realm called hell through another spiritual gateway called death.

Take note of the legal manner in which we travel between the physical and the spiritual realms, through the gifts of birth and death. This is why we cannot see the manifestation of God and His angels when they are ever present in our lives. The two realms are conjoined, but sin is a barrier.

The vortices of birth and death are the only means of entry and exit. It is a wall that we cannot ascend. When God wipes away sin, He will eradicate this barrier and we will dwell together for all of eternity. This is how, why, and when the New Jerusalem descends out of heaven from God and abides on the earth with man. (Revelation 21:10) The physical and the spiritual realms will become one.

Let's return to our sequence of events. Jesus is resurrected from hell and death, while leaving the sin of all mankind in the throes of hell, which is a different and separate realm from heaven. He ascends back to His divine position, seated at the right hand of God. He sends the Holy Spirit to fill you and guide you back to Him. All those who follow are cleansed of their sin and spiritually reunited with God through the infilling of the Holy Spirit the moment they accept Christ. We reign forever with Christ throughout all of eternity.

Logically speaking, what is the best way for God to accomplish this? What is the most logical way for Him to enter the realm of the natural? The answer is to create you in His image. Why? God knew from the very beginning of time what man would do and how He would need to rectify the problem. God knew before millisecond number one of the universe that the man He was going to create would rebel and sin against Him. He knew the end from the beginning.

Therefore, He also knew before millisecond number one of the universe that the method of redemption He chose was for Him to physically enter the realm of the natural to redeem mankind from sin and that He would make His home within you by filling you with His own Spirit. So what does He do? He does what is most logical and simple from *His* perspective, not ours. He creates that very same man to be like Him. He creates the man in His own image. Thus when redemption time came, He simply needed to put a body around His ever-ready Spirit and enter the earth through Mary's womb. Wow! Do you find that to be as mind-blowing as I do?

Contrary to popular belief, God does not like to complicate things. He is very practical and will always use the best and least complicated solution from *His* point of view. His perspective is better than ours. When viewed through His eyes, it makes perfect sense. This is how and why Jesus is *"…the image of the invisible God."* (Colossians 1:15) This is how and why in Christ *"…dwells all the fullness of the Godhead bodily."* (Colossian 2:9) This is how and why Hebrews 1:3 can state that Jesus is *"…the brightness of His glory and the **express image of His person**…."*

Do you remember when I stated that in a blood covenant the two parties would make an incision and commingle their blood? Jesus *is* the incision between God and humanity. Through His veins ran the blood of both God and man. In Christ, God inter-mingled His own blood with ours. When He spilled it to the ground, He sealed the New Covenant forever. His desire is to be forever connected to us.

One day, if you are truly willing, you will reign with Him in the everlasting light of the New Jerusalem. So stop making those empty promises; grab hold of God culture by moving from "promise to covenant" and propel yourself into eternity. Forever is at hand.

— CHAPTER 6 —

What's In a Name?

What's in a name? Scientists have recently discovered that something inside your psyche occurs when hearing the sound of your own name. It causes an immensely positive response. Hearing our names causes a response of familiarity. It leads to intimacy. Those who continually call your name are always those who know you best. They are the people you are in relationship with. In fact, many people actually become offended when someone either forgets or calls them by the wrong name.

I believe God has the same type of response when we call out His name as well. After all, it is God who implanted this response within us. It is God who created us in His image. Just as we love hearing our own names, God loves hearing His name too. Therefore, I believe we are about to embark upon a subject that is widely overlooked by the average person but, nevertheless, is of immense importance to the Almighty. It is an enormous part of God culture.

I am referring to the name(s) of God. You'll notice in the previous chapters that I have used quite a few different names and/or titles when addressing His Holiness. I must impart to you that it is imperative to address God properly. If you have ever traveled to a different country, you will notice that they may have names that sound quite unfamiliar, and perhaps even strange to your ears. The further the culture is from yours, the stranger the names seem to become to the point of not even being able to pronounce some of them. In fact, when you call someone, they may not even understand you due to your mispronunciation and accent. Do you realize you have been doing the same thing to God? Your unfamiliarity with Him is immediately present to His ears.

God and Christ are a description of what He is, but that does not necessarily tell you *who* He is. When you meet someone do you say to them, "Hey, man or woman, come here"? Perhaps when you are angry, but is that not an incredibly rude way of greeting someone, especially if you have just met or are not very close to him or her? Yet we do this to Yahweh with nearly every prayer we pray.

According to Webster's dictionary, God is defined as: The one Supreme Being, the creator and ruler of the universe. No doubt that is an accurate description; but if you are Muslim, you believe that is Allah. If you are a Jew or a Christian, you believe that is Yahweh. If you are a Scientologist, maybe you think it is L. Ron Hubbard. If you are Hindu, Buddhist, or some New Age religion, perhaps it is you or even a multitude of others.

Who Are You?

If I were to ask, "Who are you?", no doubt I would receive various answers that would describe you. Interestingly enough, however, is that no single characterization can sufficiently describe your true identity. We are simply too limited by language. Perhaps you are a mother or a father, a doctor, a lawyer, a carpenter, a Christian or a Jew, an athlete, a scholar … you get my point. All of these things may describe who and what you are; but they may also describe a plethora of other people as well. There may be an infinite number of people who describe themselves just as you do.

So what is it that allows me to identify one from another, particularly if I am unable to see you? Perhaps you are filling out a job application or something. How can I begin to sort folks out?

It's simple. It all starts with your name. Believe it or not, your name can reveal quite a bit about who you are. It may tell me your ethnic background. It may disclose your race, and it may even tell me if you are young or old. Chances are, a woman named Dorothy or Edith will be older than a woman named Sidney or Ashley.

How about if you are a man and your name is Hunter or Jared? Chances are, and of course it is not always accurate, that you are younger than Ralph or Archie. What if you have two men, one is named Smith and one is named Patel? You are most likely dealing with a Caucasian and someone of Indian descent. The main problem occurs when you have several applications with the name John Smith. I personally know two folks named Eric Johnson. They may even have the same birthday. This obviously makes it quite simple to mistake one for the other.

A Case of Mistaken Identity

It is quite common today to fall prey to identity theft throughout the world we live in. In fact, it is so common that we have developed all kinds of security measures to protect ourselves from being impersonated and robbed. Likewise, I believe that God's identity has been stolen as well. He has suffered from a case of mistaken identity for years. I would venture to say for centuries and perhaps even millennia.

I will give you an example that I know very well. My wife is from the island nation of Indonesia. If you are a Muslim in Indonesia, your God is named Allah. But guess what? If you are a Christian in Indonesia, your God is also named Allah. This is a result of the Biblical translators attempting to ease the ear of the Muslim. You may be thinking, however, "So what? There is only one God. What's the difference in what you call Him? We all worship the same God. Do you think He really cares whether or not you call Him Allah or Jehovah or whatever?"

The simple truth is that this thought process, which has run rampant throughout the modern world, is simply untrue. It is counter to God culture. Allah is not and cannot be the same God as Jehovah. Think about this logically for a moment. Jehovah, in both the Old and New Testaments of the Bible, says that Jesus is His Son and that He has a Spirit, the Holy Spirit. Allah denies this truth. Jehovah is described as a triune God, three natures—Father, Son and Holy Spirit—independent in their administrations over mankind and the universe, although not separate, but equal in honor and glory, encompassing the nature of one God (See Isaiah 48:16).

Allah however has only one nature as the Supreme Ruler over creation. He does not interact with mankind and does not offer a personal relationship. There is no Holy Spirit given to be the helper, teacher, and guide for mankind, and no Son given as our Savior from sin. He simply implements the rules and pronounces judgment when they are not upheld. So let me ask you: Can these two be the same? Will the real God please stand up?! Which *is* the true nature of God? How can the true God distinguish Himself from the imposter? It is quite simple… He has a name(s).

Allow me to address the question of, "Who cares what you call Him?" with Scripture. I will let God answer that question and you can judge for yourself whether or not you feel His name is important to Him, and if, in fact, addressing Him correctly is of any importance *to you.* Keep in mind that God has always identified Himself and His reputation to the world through the actions of the people He chooses as His own. Check out what follows:

"Moreover the Word of the Lord came to me (the prophet Ezekiel) *saying, 'Son of man, when the house of Israel dwelt in their own land, they defiled it by their own ways and deeds; to Me their way was like the uncleanness of a woman in her customary impurity. Therefore I poured out my fury on them for the blood they had shed on the land, and for their idols with which they had defiled it. So I*

scattered them among the nations, and they were dispersed (by being taken captive) *throughout the countries; I judged them according to their ways and deeds."'*
—Ezekiel 36:16-19

During Ezekiel's time, the Israelites had completely abandoned God culture and it made Him ill. In God's eyes, their culture had become defiled. I don't have to tell you that this was not going to turn out well. It never does. If you are going to be associated with the name of God, you must be in control of your ways and deeds. You must be conscious of God culture. You must act with dignity and discipline and act in accordance with *His* ways and not yours. If you do not, you fall into the following category.

"When they (the Israelites) *came to the nations, wherever they went,* **they profaned My holy name**—*when they* (gentiles) *said of them, 'These are the people of the Lord, and yet they have gone out of His land.* **But I had concern for My holy name,** *which the house of Israel had profaned among the nations wherever they went'".*
—Ezekiel 36:20-21

In case you feel God is not speaking to you but only to the Jewish people by using the phrase "house of Israel", consider the following: if you believe in Jesus Christ, you belong to the house of Israel. *"Therefore it is of faith that it might be according to grace, so that the promise might be to **all the seed,** not only to those who are of the law, but also to those who are of the faith of Abraham, who is the father of us all…"* (Romans 4:16)

In essence, if you are a believer in Jesus Christ, regardless of your denomination (Baptist, Catholic, Lutheran, etc.), then you are the seed of Abraham and, therefore, a member of the house of Israel. Depending on how you live your life, you may be profaning the holy name of God.

However, if you are not a believer in Christ and you are not a Jew, you cannot be profaning His name because you simply do not belong to Him … yet. He wants you. He is offering to be your Father but you must believe in Him and His way, and His way is Christ. *"Nor is there salvation in any other, for there is no other* **name** *under heaven given among men by which we must be saved."* (Acts 4:12)

Let's continue on in Ezekiel. *"Therefore say to the house of Israel, 'Thus says the Lord God: I do not do this for your sake, O house of Israel,* **but for My holy name's sake,** *which you have profaned among the nations wherever you went.* **And I will sanctify** (which means to set apart, so that there is no mistaking Him) **My great name,** *which has been profaned among the nations, which you have profaned in their midst; and the nations shall know that I am the Lord,' says the Lord God, 'when I am hallowed* **in you** *before* **their** *eyes.* (A man's introduction to God has always been through the behavior of His people.)

For I will take you from among the nations and gather you out of all countries, and bring you into your own land (this may have begun in 1947 with the creation, or re-creation of Israel and the subsequent and continuous immigration of the Jewish people back to the Holy Land*). Then I will sprinkle clean water on you, and you shall be clean; I will cleanse you from all your filthiness and your idols. I will give you a new heart and a new spirit within you; I will take the heart of stone out of your flesh, and give you a heart of flesh.* **I will put My Spirit within you** *and cause you to walk in My statutes, and you will keep My judgments and do them. Then you shall dwell in the land that I gave to your fathers; you shall be My people and I will be your God. I will deliver you from all your uncleanness. I will call for the grain and multiply it, and bring no famine upon you. ...* **Not for your sake do I do this,'** *says the Lord God, 'let it be known to you.'"* (Ezekiel 36:22-32)

So let me ask that question again. Is God's name important to Him? Is His reputation important, how about His culture? Is it important to acknowledge Him properly? Is His name important to *us?* You bet it is!

Not only is it important, it is imperative for you to know. Hey, your kids do not go to another man for sustenance. God does not want His glory going to another, just as you do not want another man raising your children. It is a child's father who provides for him or her. Another man will not. Therefore, you acknowledge your father with respect and by his rightful name and/or term of endearment.

Unfaithful

I watched something interesting on TV prior to writing this. It was a show regarding unfaithful spouses. There was this woman who cheated on her husband and wound up pregnant. In the birthing room, she gives birth to a young, healthy African American child. The only problem was that both she and her husband were Asian, and guess what? She didn't tell him about the affair. To make a long story short, the husband eventually forgave the wife but he could not deal with having the child around. Two months after the birth of the child, she gave him up for adoption.

What I found particularly interesting is the marriage counselor whom they sought out stated that in his thirty-five years of practice he had only seen the "parents" keep this type of baby once. In all his years of practice when confronted with this situation, the unnatural father was only willing to rear up that child one time and that particular couple remains in turmoil to the present day.

After nine years, the "father" remains resentful toward that poor child, and it is and always will be a bone of contention between them. Why is that? The child does not belong to the father. The child does not bear his resemblance or his name. A child simply does not go to another man for sustenance. That simply is not our culture. No matter how hard they try, they simply cannot get over the betrayal. The daily reminder of the adulterous affair is just too much.

Is it any different with God who *is* our Father? Have you gone to the "world" for support instead of going to the Father? How's that working out? I'll bet you feel completely fulfilled, right? Then why are you reading this book? If you are searching for wholeness in a "world" without God, you will never be filled.

How about the devil, will you go to him for support? Will you bear *his* resemblance and name? Oh, he will certainly agree, but there is a hell of a price to be paid. Pun intended. Perhaps you already have and don't even realize it. Allow me to let you in on a little secret. Anything sought outside of God's presence and/or will is of the devil. This is also counter to God culture.

God equates it to being in an adulterous affair against Him. If it keeps you from God, it is not of God. Always remember and analyze your life according to that very simple principle because Satan has tried to steal God's name, His reputation, and His family ever since he was cast out of heaven. He has become quite adept at it, and he is more than happy to temporarily fill your needs and wants in exchange for destroying your soul.

Therefore, I thank God every day that He is not a man like you and me. When you come to Him, He quite simply places a new spirit in you. He throws the old one in the trash where it belongs and resurrects a new one in you, perfect according to His definition and one with Him without sin.

In essence, you are reborn out of the illegitimate adulterous situation you flaunted before Him for so long and grafted into righteousness through the blood of Jesus Christ. Not only does He forgive your transgressions, He actually removes them. Therefore, He no longer has to gaze upon that daily reminder of the spiritually adulterous life you have lived for so long. He purifies you and restores you back into His image (or resemblance). You now begin to take on *His* characteristics along with *His* name and, yes, ultimately, His reputation and culture.

Terms of Endearment

Let's begin by taking a look at His name, or more accurately, His names. Do not be surprised that God has different names that describe different characteristics. My name is John Naphor. My wife calls me Hun, short for Honey. Sometimes she calls me John or Napes. I respond to all three. My kids call me Dad. My friends also call me Napes. The neighborhood children call me Mr. Naphor. My nieces and nephews call me Uncle John.

I am the same guy but each name, nickname, and term of endearment is based on a particular relationship that person has with me. Each person approaches me for different reasons. Those calling me Dad approach me for sustenance, protection, guidance and affection. My wife approaches Honey for intimacy. Those approaching Napes do so for friendship and camaraderie. Mr. Naphor and Uncle John are terms of respect. All are accurate but each describes a unique relationship. The beauty with God is that we can approach Him for all these things and more. He is all sufficient.

The Prince of Egypt

I would like to begin this discussion in the wilderness of Midian when Moses has the famous burning bush encounter. For many years, I found this revelation of the Almighty to be a bit strange. It simply didn't make sense. Let's have a look and then I'll explain.

"Now Moses was tending the flocks of Jethro his father-in-law, the priest of Midian." (Exodus 3:1) I must state here that Moses was a bit of a confused Hebrew at this point and, considering his life circumstances, it sort of makes sense. He was born a Hebrew in Egypt. However, in order to avoid his slaughter by the Egyptians as a result of Pharoah's decree, his mom floated him down the Nile River in a little ark-like basket. He just happened to be found and adopted by Pharaoh's daughter. Gee, what a bummer! While all the Hebrew babies were killed and anyone above two years old or so were slaves presumably building the pyramids, ol' Moses grows up as the Prince of Egypt in Pharaoh's court.

However, God put a little bit of a twist in the situation because Pharaoh's daughter did not know how to and did not have any real desire to raise the child. I am pretty sure she equated it to saving a puppy, so she brought a Hebrew nanny with her who, unbeknownst to the young royal maiden, just happened to be Moses' actual birth mother. I know; it's a God thing. Actually, as you will find out shortly it's a God culture thing. So as Moses is living as royalty in the most advanced civilization of the then-known world, his mother is continuously teaching him the ways, traditions and religion of the Hebrew people.

Naturally he has somewhat of a bond with these folks, but undoubtedly he is following the worship of the false gods of the Egyptians. In essence, Moses is leading a double life. Sound familiar? Perhaps you have been doing the same. At various times throughout my life, I most certainly have.

One day, Moses sees an Egyptian slave master beating a Hebrew slave and he simply cannot take any more. So he rises up, looks around, and kills the man's abuser. Wow, what a great and noble deed! You would think he would have won their favor. He should have been revered by the Hebrew people, right? They should have been writing and singing hymns about him, like "The Legend of Moses, the Hidden Hebrew."

But wait, not so fast. The next day he sees two Hebrews fighting one another. He steps in between them and asks a completely logical question. *"Why are you striking your companion?"* Most likely he is expecting to hear, "Hey guys, everything is OK. 'Moses the Great' is here. Let's sing his theme song; he'll help us."

Is that the response he encounters? Unfortunately, or fortunately, depending upon your "now vs. forever" perspective, that is not the welcome he receives. Instead, he is slapped in the face with, *"Who made you a prince and a judge over us? Do you intend to kill me as you killed the Egyptian?"* (Exodus 2:14)

Uh oh! Now Moses is freaking out. He thought no one saw. He thought there was no way the Hebrews would squeal on him. He had forgotten one thing. The Hebrews did not know he was Hebrew. They thought he was Pharaoh's son. Obviously this particular gentleman did not care if he lived or died, based on the way he addressed the Prince of Egypt.

So Moses panics. He knows that he is merely an adopted son of Pharaoh and, most likely, about to be put to death for killing an Egyptian citizen. You see, Pharaoh had a naturally born son as well, Ramses II. Although Pharaoh may have loved Moses as one of his own, based on Moses' reaction, he and Ramses II obviously did not receive the same treatment. So he flees across the desert.

Deliverer

Fast forward forty or so years and that leads us to the burning bush incident where we find this confused "Egyptian looking" Hebrew. He obviously had no idea who his God was based upon the fact that he is now on the lam and is living with and married to the daughter of the heathen priest of Midian, who also happened to be a relative of his. And you thought you were messed up! God, however, has not given up on him and actually has a plan for this outcast fleeing from society. Things are about to change.

"Now it happened in the process of time that the king of Egypt died. Then the children of Israel groaned because of their bondage, and they cried out; and their cry came up to God because of their bondage. So God heard their groaning, and God remembered His covenant with Abraham, with Isaac, and with Jacob. And God looked upon the children of Israel and acknowledged them."
—Exodus 2:23-25

In other words, Jehovah remembered God culture. May I ask a question at this point? Have you cried out to God? If you have not, you are unknowingly living the life of a slave. What I mean by this is that you are living as a slave of sin, which causes you to give in to the lusts of your flesh.

When you make Christ your Lord, you become a child of the covenant, just as the children of Israel are, and God cannot look away from your cries. He will not look away from your groaning. When you make your voice heard in His courts, He will acknowledge you. Just like Moses, you will have your very own burning bush incident, only you do not need Moses as your deliverer. God has sent you Christ. The beauty within this opportunity is that it is always available to you. God will always hear your cries. It is never too late to enter God culture. Until you have breathed your last breath you have not lost the chance to connect with Him and receive Him.

Tell Them I Exist

Let's get back to Moses for a moment because we are about to be introduced, by name, to the maker of the universe. *"Now Moses was tending the flock ... And he led the flock back to the desert, and came to Horeb, the mountain of God. And the Angel of the Lord* (who, as previously stated, many theologians including myself believe to be the pre-incarnate Christ) *appeared to him in a flame of fire from the midst of a bush. So he looked, and behold the bush was burning with fire, but the bush was not consumed. Then Moses said, 'I will now turn aside and see this great sight, why the bush does not burn.'*

"So when the Lord saw that he turned aside to look, God called to him from the midst of the bush and said, 'Moses, Moses!' And he said, 'Here I am.'

"Then He said, 'Do not draw near this place. Take your sandals off your feet, for the place where you stand is holy ground.' Moreover He said, 'I am the God of your fathers—the God of Abraham, the God of Isaac, and the God of Jacob.' And Moses hid his face, for he was afraid to look upon God.

"And the Lord said, 'I have surely seen the oppression of My people ... Come now, therefore, and I will send you to Pharaoh that you may bring my people, the children of Israel, out of Egypt.'

"But Moses said to God, 'Who am I that I should go to Pharaoh, and that I should bring the children of Israel out of Egypt?'

*"So He said, 'I will certainly be with you. And this shall be a sign.' Then Moses said to God, 'Indeed, when I come to the children of Israel and say to them, 'The God of your fathers has sent me to you,' and they say to me, **'What is His name?'** what shall I say to them?'*

"And God said to Moses, 'I AM WHO I AM.' And He said, 'Thus you shall say to the children of Israel, 'I AM has sent me to you.'"

At first glance, this really seems like a strange response on the part of God. "I AM sent me?" What is *that?* What in the world does *that* mean? I asked for your name and you answered me with a present tense verb? I told you names from different cultures can be quite strange. This is certainly no exception.

What is extremely interesting about this response is its meaning in the original Hebrew language. The verb AM in this instance is a translation of the Hebrew word **hayah**, pronounced *haw-yaw*. It means to exist. The verb connotes that God's name is not static, but active. It is a union of being, becoming, and acting. This means that God has the ability to be, become, and do whatever it is that pleases Him and whatever it is that we need Him for, including, but not limited to, becoming the Perfect Man in the person of Jesus Christ for the purpose of salvation.

So when Moses asked, "Who should I say sent me," God replied, "Tell them I Exist sent you. Moses, tell them I exist! Tell them I am about to do something mind blowing." This makes perfect sense due to the fact that the Israelites have now been enslaved and persecuted for some four hundred years. Let's be honest, we question the existence of God if He does not answer our prayer in a week.

Listen to what the author of the Book of Hebrews had to say about this very same subject: "*...but without faith it is impossible to please Him, for he who comes to God must believe that He is, and that He is a rewarder of those who diligently seek Him.*" (Hebrews 11:6) Isn't God saying the same thing here? "If you are to come to Me, you must first and foremost believe that I exist, that I AM." Therefore, the first revelation God wanted to give to the people, the first representation of His holy name, was to declare that He exists. He was about to prove it. He will do the same for you, if you let Him.

Most of us have seen the movie *The Ten Commandments* and know the end of the story. Moses returns and performs all sorts of signs and wonders in front of Pharaoh. God sends the ten plagues to Pharaoh and eventually we are led to the parting of the Red Sea; but why is God so concerned about whether or not the people believe? Let's refer back to Hebrews 11:6 and then I will share an incident from the life of Jesus Christ which illustrates this point. Hebrews 11:6 begins by saying, "*...but without faith it is impossible to please Him...*"

If you have not already noticed, I have a deep belief in having an understanding of the language, especially those "religious" idioms, that appear within the pages of the Bible or any other religious writing, for that matter. This is certainly one such instance because the Scripture is prefaced by the word "faith." If you do not believe what God says, it is not just difficult but *impossible* to please Him. "Impossible to please" is a veritably strong unit of communication.

"Impossible," as it is used here, comes from the Greek word "*adunatos*" and its definition is "unable," meaning you cannot, no matter how hard you try, please God without first believing that He exists. Think about that for a moment. Would your own father be pleased if you accused him of being an absentee Dad, or if you simply refused to acknowledge his presence when he is with you? I think not. So why is it any different with God?

Couple that with the word "please," which in this instance is not a means of being polite, but rather means to "fully gratify." The above Scripture clearly states that if you do not come to God in faith, you cannot gratify Him. William Newton Clark said, "Faith is daring the soul to go beyond what the eyes can see." In other words, without faith, God is left unsatisfied, and if He is, so are you. Are you beginning to understand why you feel empty without Him?

Hebrews 11:6 goes on to say that *"he who comes to God **must**,"* as in not optional, *"believe that He is…"* You must believe that he exists, and *"that He is a **rewarder** of those who **diligently** seek Him."* God is a rewarder. That is part of His culture. He loves to give gifts. It is who He is.

But, and for some people there always seems to be a "big but" in the way, He has a condition for giving out His rewards. You must not just seek but *diligently* seek Him. The word diligent means "to be constant in effort." So number one, you must believe He exists, and, number two, you must be constant in your pursuit of Him. Then He will reward you. With what? I don't know. That is between you and Him, but He certainly knows exactly what drives you so let Him know your true motive. There is no need to try to fool Him or you.

Here is what happens when you leave any one part of this equation out. Here is that incident from the life of Jesus that I mentioned earlier. *"When He* (Jesus) *had come to His own country, He taught them in their synagogue, so that they were astonished and said, 'Where did this man get this wisdom and these mighty works? Is this not the carpenter's son? Is not His mother called Mary and His brothers James, Joses, Simon, and Judas? And His sisters, aren't they all with us? Where then did this man get all these things?' So they were offended at Him. Now he did not do many mighty works there **because of their unbelief.**"* (Matthew 13: 54-58)

This and the other Gospel accounts of it are perhaps the only place in the Word of God that we see Jesus' power appear to be limited. Take note of how He was being referred to as well, "this man," "the carpenter's son," no one ever said His name. Is it just me or does this sound rude to you as well?

However, it does not say that he *could* not do *any* works; it says He *did* not do *many* works. We know that He did some works; He just did not do many. I would venture to guess that those whom He helped probably had no idea who He was or were foreigners to Nazareth. Why? They must not have known the culture. Those complaining all knew Him, and this was His hometown. In their minds, Nazareth could only produce ordinary people. *"And Nathanael said to him, 'Can anything good come out of Nazareth?'"* (John 1:46)

They knew His mother, His brothers, His sisters, and, as a result, they just could not believe He could be someone special. Perhaps you see yourself and your own hometown in a similar manner. "Could anything special come from..." you fill in the blank. It actually says they were astonished at His teachings in the synagogue. To put it bluntly, they simply did not connect with Him and, just like you and me, they put up a wall between them and God. They were separated from God culture.

Without being arrogant, may I say that there will be quite a few people who will be astonished that I wrote this book, and for the very same reason. They know my mistakes. They know my shortcomings. They have seen me get angry. They have seen me get drunk, and they have even seen me get scared.

They will have the exact same reaction. "Isn't that John, the one I used to party with? Isn't that Ed and Kathy's son? Isn't his brother Ed, and his sisters, don't I know who they are? I used to hang out with him. Where did this come from?" Many of them will be offended at my newfound "righteousness" and not receive the message of this book simply because they know who I used to be and cannot accept who I have become. I am no longer a part of the world's culture.

It was no different with Jesus. They did not, would not, and could not accept that He was who He said He was. They did not believe in His name, which has a specific meaning that we will cover shortly. As a result of their disbelief, they did not believe that He was their deliverer and would not fully gratify Him; therefore, He did not do many mighty works there. His reward was with Him (Revelation 22:12) but He would not give it to those who were unwilling to receive it.

God's first revelation to you will always be that He exists. Only then, when you have been exposed to the Master of the universe, can you even comprehend how broken you truly are and that He is the only one who can fix you. That will cause you to fall to your knees and call upon the mighty name of Jesus. All of God's other attributes, which we will cover in part, are meaningless until you have come to this point. So let's look at the name of Jesus, *"for there is no other name under heaven given among men by which we must be saved."* (Acts 4:12)

God Is Salvation

The name Jesus is the Greek version of the name Joshua, which is actually Yeshua in Hebrew. Its literal meaning is "God is salvation." Now Acts 4:12 makes sense. Of course it is the only name under heaven by which we must be saved. Who else is salvation but God alone? Therefore, what other name can save you? I certainly cannot. Neither can your parents, brothers, sisters, pastor, priest, friends, relatives, mullah, rabbi or any other. It is Jesus alone who can save you.

Remember, the word "salvation" comes from the Greek word "soteria" which means deliverance, preservation and safety as well as the saving of one's spirit and soul from eternal damnation.

Let's visit some of God's other names in order to gain an understanding of His attributes. This will allow you to understand who He actually is, in addition to being your Savior and Master of the universe. You will now gain an understanding of how He is soteria and how and why He desires to relate to you on a personal level. It is not what He wants; it is who He is! You can change what you want but you cannot change who you are. God can but you cannot. Since God is unchanging (Malachi 3:6), pay close attention to what follows.

Elohim

Let's begin with the first mention of the word "God" that appears in the Bible. It comes from Genesis Chapter 1:1 and it is translated into English as "God." The original Hebrew name is Elohim and Genesis 1:1 actually reads as follows: *"In the beginning Elohim created…"*

Interestingly enough, Elohim is a plural word and its meaning is that of a governor or magistrate. What I find to be revelatory in this instance is that the very first usage of God is not the name "El", which is the singular form of God with the connotation of unparalleled strength. The first usage is "Elohim", thus imparting first and foremost the plurality of God's nature and His ability to manage and govern everything in eternity.

We then see the Spirit of God hovering over the face of the deep (Genesis 1:2) and later see God literally, in a physical sense, "walking" in the Garden of Eden with Adam and Eve (Genesis 3:8). Revealed within the very first chapters of the Bible is the triune nature of God, and ultimately His will to be personally a part of mankind's life.

Elohim is participatory. He was an active part of Adam and Eve's life, and He wants to be an active part of yours as well. Thus every time you speak the name Elohim, it should remind you of the fact that the Lord personally wants to be a part of your life and "walk" with you on a daily basis. He wants you to play an active part in His culture.

El Shaddai

As we read on in the Book of Genesis, it is not long before we are introduced to El Shaddai. Shaddai means "the all-powerful One." "El" means God and, as stated earlier, connotes strength, thus reinforcing the immense and unmatched power of the one and only living God, El Shaddai. This is how He revealed Himself to Abraham when He was about to make a ninety-year old barren woman pregnant. That makes sense, doesn't it? "I am El Shaddai." "I am the Supreme power over all of Creation. Causing a barren woman to become pregnant? No problem. I am all sufficient in all things." That is how Abraham knew God. How do you know Him?

Jehovah

We must realize that throughout the Bible, God is continuously progressing in His revelation to mankind. The same is true of His names. When we get to the Book of Exodus, we find God deepening His proclamation by using the name Jehovah and/or Yahweh. Many of the Jews have shortened the spelling of Yahweh to YHWH, removing all of the vowels, and thus making the pronunciation of His name impossible due to their reverence of the all-powerful God of the infinity and beyond—and you thought it was Buzz Lightyear, ha ha!

What is really cool about the names Jehovah and Yahweh is that they are synonymous, meaning "He causes to become." Wow! Think about the power in that name. God causes the universe to become. He causes the stars to become; he causes the plants, the animals, the fish to become; He causes man to become; He causes everything to become, and ultimately He causes *you* to become. My my my… If you will just let Him, He will cause you to become everything you have ever wanted to be. Even more importantly, He will cause you to become everything *He* wants you to be; in fact, everything that you were created to be. That is true perfection.

With that in mind, let's have a look at some of the variations on the name Jehovah and exactly what He causes to become when you allow *Him* to be a part of your life. We will start with Jehovah Shalom. The Hebrew word "shalom" is translated into English as "peace." Shalom is much more than peace, which we would define as tranquility. It is a similar word to salvation in its meaning, in that nothing is missing and nothing is broken in your life. You are whole.

Jehovah Shalom is the God of peace. He is the God of wholeness. In fact, if you couple that with the meaning of Jehovah, He is the causer of peace in your life. He is the cause of nothing missing and nothing being broken. That applies to everything you can think of and a whole lot of which you cannot. *"Now to Him who is able to do exceedingly abundantly above all that we ask or think, according to the power that works in us…"* (Ephesians 3:20) Do not allow your lack of foresight to be a hindrance, however, because Jehovah is omnipotent, omniscient and omnipresent. He's got your back! God culture contains not just sufficiency, but an overflowing of abundance.

Let's contrast that discovery with who you may have previously thought God was, as well as, what you thought He was the *cause* of. He is the cause of peace and not pain. He will allow you to experience pain. He will even allow you to experience suffering, if that is what it takes to bring you to salvation. I would almost guarantee that if all you are experiencing is chaos, suffering and pain in your life, it is not Jehovah Shalom at work. It is certainly not God culture that you are experiencing.

So who is option two? I believe you have answered well. There are only two other possibilities: you, Satan, or perhaps both. You will have to figure that one out on your own. It's time for a gut check, my friend. God is love, not pain.

Now that you have come to this realization and you have ejected the adversary from your life, it is time to call upon Jehovah Nisi. Jehovah Nisi means "the Lord my banner." That is who He is as I write this book. This discourse is the banner that God has been in my life. My aim is to glorify Him, to shout about His goodness, and to teach all those willing to listen who He truly is. He has redeemed my life from destruction (Psalm 91). He has given me a name and a family. He is the cause of my business and all that is good in my life. He introduced me to my wife, created my children, and has patiently revealed Himself to the stubborn, stiff-necked man that I can so often be. He has caused me to become a new creation, complete in His will and perfect in His eyes, the only eyes that matter. As a result, I will shout about His goodness from the rooftops. He has become my banner! He is the cause of my praise.

All that I am and have is a result of Him. Unbeknownst to me at the time, He has always been Jehovah Jireh to me as well. Jehovah Jireh means "the Lord my provider." No matter what is going on in my life, He is always there. In good times and in bad, when I am angry and when I am happy, He is always there. He never lets me go hungry or naked or destitute, even when I rebel against Him. He *is* my every need and He wants to be yours too.

I cannot escape Him. He is always there. He is Jehovah Shammah, "the Lord is there." That is what Jehovah Shammah means. I will never forget when I was a teenager amidst a drug buy gone bad. We walked into an apartment where we were immediately ambushed by men who were pointing guns at our heads. This was one of the scariest days of my life but Jehovah Shammah was there. He calmed the situation and I went on to live another day. He knew my purpose and the end of all of my days. I find it comforting to know that whether I live or die, he is there. He is Jehovah Shammah.

Finally, as this is not intended to be an exhaustive list, I will end with Jehovah Shiloh, "the Lord my rest." He causes rest in my life. He is refreshing. As a result of outside circumstances, I was very stressed when I began to pen this chapter. As always, He has caused me to no longer feel such anxiety. Why should I, with Him on my side? Even better said, how *could I* with Him on my side? The Lord is with me. He is also with you.

The Lord Works in Mysterious Ways

In closing, it is quite interesting to look at the progression of God's names. There are five main progressions to the revelation of who God is through the divulgence of His name. He begins as Elohim, the Governor and Magistrate of the universe.

I feel most people's idea of how God operates, "The Lord works in mysterious ways," is completely invalid. That is not God culture; it is laziness. That phrase does not appear in Scripture, and it is certainly not a Biblical principle. The truth is that when you begin to understand God and His ways, you will find that He is completely logical. The problem is that we cannot always see what He is doing because He always operates from the perspective of foresight, which is an ability that none of us mere mortals have.

I would not say that He is mysterious. In fact, I believe the opposite is true. When you begin to diligently seek Him, He will reveal Himself to you without hesitation. It is like a little game of "hide and seek." Hide and seek is not a mystery; we all know the rules. It is just a matter of being diligent enough to unveil the location of the "hider."

The same is true when studying the names of God. Elohim, as an example, is a perfectly logical name when you realize that God is revealing the process of creation when this name is unveiled. He is letting you know that not only does He possess the power to create, but He also possesses the strength to personally manage, participate in, and unite with His creation in a physical, spiritual and emotional sense.

Once this is established, the Lord progresses to El Shaddai, the Supreme Power of the universe Who is all sufficient and without limitations. Consider what God is about to do when He reveals His name to be El Shaddai. He is aiming to perform a miracle. For the first time, He is about to cause a woman who has been barren her entire life to become pregnant. Only the all-powerful God who is limited by nothing, no matter what the circumstance, is able perform such feats. Once this precedent is established, He really outdoes Himself by causing the Virgin Mary to become pregnant with the Savior of mankind.

Has God said or done anything illogical up to this point, notwithstanding the hilarity of His power? His immensity pales us in comparison. In fact, it reduces us to nothing. That is purposeful. With this realization, it becomes apparent as to how much we truly need Him.

When the next name is revealed, we are introduced to the existence of Jehovah or Yahweh, the One who causes to become. Once again, this is perfectly logical when one realizes that God was dealing with Moses and causing Moses, the insecure stutterer, to defy Pharaoh, the most powerful man on Earth, and become the miracle-working deliverer of the entire nation of Israel. In fact, God was actually causing Israel to become an independent nation. He was delivering them out of their bondage, thus causing them to be free to worship Him in the wilderness and ultimately amidst the freedom of the Promised Land. He was creating God culture.

The wilderness was never the ultimate destination for the people of God. Keep that in mind if you feel that you are there right now. God's goal for creation and mankind has always been and will always be oneness with Him, but not in our current wilderness-driven states. God never intended for his people to die in the wilderness.

Thus we are introduced to the name of the Redeemer, Jesus—"God is salvation." In the name of Jesus, mankind is delivered from the wilderness of sin and delivered into everlasting life in perfect harmony with the name of our final revelation, our Father, Abba. Abba means Daddy in Hebrew. In our Father, we find unconditional love, protection, sustenance, and everything necessary for the everlasting life of God's most spectacular creation, mankind. "Father" is the ultimate revelation of who God is. It is the complete definition of God culture. It is His holiest name.

So as I end this amazing little chapter, I will ask one final question, and it happens to be the one I asked in the beginning of the chapter. What's in a name? My friends, since God is salvation, *my* "final answer" is... forever!

— CHAPTER 7 —

Mercy

I believe mercy is without a doubt the most misunderstood attribute of God, yet it is one of the primary elements of God culture. The majority of the world, many Christians included, presume that God is some colossal ogre just sitting upon His throne looking for someone to either abuse or mess with. Then when He feels like it, or if He finds someone that He particularly likes, He will bless that person. That is *not* who God is.

They act as if He is an evil puppet master, pulling the strings and laughing as the lives of His "puppets" fall into ruin and shambles, unwilling or, even worse, unable to do anything about it. As a result, *"from the days of John the Baptist until now the kingdom of heaven suffers violence, and the violent take it by force."* (Matthew 11:12) Incredibly, many misguided people from quite possibly every religion on Earth actually believe they are doing God's will while committing horrendous acts of violence in His name. By doing so, they unwittingly place themselves in direct opposition to God culture.

In truth, world cultures always have and always will be incredibly violent. *"And you will hear of wars and rumors of wars. **See that you are not troubled**; for all these things **must** come to pass, but the end is not yet."* (Matthew 24:6) The violent will always take the world by force. That is just the way things are and, as always, a quick glance at the evening news or a short perusing of the Internet will quickly validate Jesus' claim.

How can we *not* be concerned for our children's futures when we see the horrors of New Town, Connecticut, and the innocent maimed and killed for simply running in a foot race, as was the case with the Boston Marathon bombings? Then there is the Middle East, which at the current moment may be affecting the psyche and perhaps even the wellbeing of the entire planet. There is no denying that the culture of mankind is irreparably violent, even in the most peaceful of nations.

Jesus, however, is not making reference to man's culture in Matthew 11:12. He is making reference to God culture suffering violence. He is referring to the kingdom of heaven being taken by force. And it is! God culture is under attack from world culture. Biblical values and Biblical world views are quickly being replaced by humanism, atheism, a complete loss of morality and theological illiteracy. By all rights, God should just blow the place to high heaven!

Yet He is not even angry. He is not surprised and He certainly has not lost control. Through it all, God still loves mankind, and as a result His judgment tarries. His immeasurable love causes Him to wait. As society completely falls by the wayside, God calls out to each individual. In love and in mercy, He awaits your return.

You will soon realize that everything God does is a result of His love, grace, and mercy. Once you understand this concept, you will have the insight to see how God has and will continue to work in your life. You will see Him in the shadows of your past, present, and future. In truth, you can never truly comprehend His goodness until you have an understanding of His mercy.

In order to experience God's mercy in action, let's go back to where it all began. Let's go back to the videotape of the Garden of Eden and visit with Adam, the first man ever created. It is in this epic narrative that we see sin take root on the earth and defile both man and nature, even to this present day. It is here that original sin alters the nature and, as a result, the culture of mankind. It is also here that we will experience the first acts of mercy from our loving Creator.

In order for you to actually experience His mercy, you must first have a change of heart as to who God is and why He acts as He does. Therefore, to begin this excursion, I must lay some foundation to the Genesis account. What most perceive to be punishment, when seen through the eyes of God, will actually turn out to be mercy. As always, His merciful acts are not just for the present condition of a man, but for all those throughout eternity. You are about to discover that mercy is also part of His "Now vs. Forever" plan. God culture is a culture of mercy. It is a cultural element of His kingdom. So are you ready? Genesis account: take one… action!

That's a Good Question

"Now the serpent was more cunning than any beast of the field which the Lord God had made." (Genesis 3:1) We begin our account not with Adam or Eve, but instead with the serpent, as it is imperative to note several issues here. First, the serpent was cunning. The word "cunning" simply means "tricky." The devil was, and still is, tricky. How else could he deceive so many? Second, the devil, having inhabited the body of a serpent, was presumably already in the garden when God placed Adam there, and, third, it is God who created him and has the ultimate power over him.

This leads us to several interesting questions that most are not prepared to or are unwilling to deal with, let alone answer. Questions such as: Why did God create evil? Why does He allow it? Does God have the power to stop it? If He loves us, why would He allow these horrible things to occur? I have been asked questions like these and others such as: Why does God allow babies to die? Why does God allow the people of Africa to starve? Why is there so much sickness, poverty, suffering etc. in the world if an all-powerful and all loving God is in control?

The inability to answer these questions has prevented millions, and perhaps even billions, from being saved. Therefore, we will spend this chapter discussing evil and answering such harrowing questions. Evil is not necessarily what you think it is, and despite what you may believe, it certainly has a purpose. The ability to deal with such matters will help prepare you to partake of the end-time harvest, which is imminent.

Questions such as these are real issues that the dying people of the world must have answered. Suffice it to say for now, that God is aware, He *is* in control, and He is able to use these situations to His, which is ultimately *our*, advantage. There is a reason and a "Now" vs. "Forever" plan in evil. For now, let's examine the circumstances leading to the sin that has created so much pain and suffering on the earth and in our own lives.

Dominion and Authority

> *"Now the serpent was more cunning than any beast of the field which the Lord God had made. And he said to the woman, 'Has God indeed said, you shall not eat of every tree of the Garden?'"*
> **—Genesis 3:1**

Before we go any further, let's examine the blessing (empowerment) given to mankind at creation. *"Then God said, 'Let Us make man in Our image, according to our likeness;* **let them have dominion** *over the fish of the sea, over the birds of the air, and over the cattle,* **over all the earth** *and over every creeping thing* (this includes serpents) *that creeps on the earth... Then God blessed them, 'Be fruitful and multiply; fill the earth* **and subdue it; have dominion** *over the fish of the sea, over the birds of the air, and over every living thing that moves on the earth.'"* (Genesis 1:26-28)

First, in order to make sure there is no misunderstanding about whom God had blessed, the above Scriptures continually use the personal pronoun "them" when describing the man being created. Therefore, the authority given to Adam at creation was not only intended, but was *actively* given to *all* of mankind throughout eternity. It was intended to be a human trait, a characteristic of man.

In today's world, we actually see the perversion of this characteristic in mankind's imperialistic nature, which has been continually manifested throughout history in the form of wars, conflicts, murders, and an array of other abuses of power. They are all a futile attempt to exercise dominion and authority over man, whom we were never given the authority to dominate.

Here is a quick note regarding the above statement: "We were never given dominion over each other." The beasts of the field, yes; the birds of the air, yes; the creeping things upon the earth, yes; but over each other—absolutely not! Only God has dominion and authority over mankind. Not even the angels of heaven do. Our attempt to oppress and dominate one another is a perversion of the dominion given to mankind at creation. We were created to live with one another in the perfect fellowship of love and harmony upon the earth.

Let's get back to the Adam situation. Do you realize that Adam actually had the authority to seize control of the situation going down in the Garden? He could have, *and should have*, immediately ousted Satan from the Garden of Eden. We will discuss why he did not, but suffice it to say at this point in time that he should have been, and in reality *was*, in control of the situation of the Garden. God had given him dominion and authority.

The word "dominion" means to dominate. Mankind was created to dominate the earth. Righteous dominion is a major aspect of God culture. Once again, we continue, even to this present day, to see this God-given ability abused and corrupted in mankind's natural inclination not only to dominate but to abuse man and earth.

What must be understood is that the correct usage of the characteristics of dominion and authority are immensely powerful and positive traits when entrusted to the right human beings. I should actually say, when entrusted to the "righteous" human beings, meaning those who are in right standing with God. However, these are traits that need to be taught to us. We naturally have the ability, but we are not born with the know-how of its proper usage. Although God has given us the ability and the inclination, He has left the responsibility of teaching the proper use of these tools to us.

When the above command of, "Be fruitful, multiply, and have dominion" was given to Adam, Eve was not even present. She had not been physically created yet. Later, as the serpent begins to question Eve, it becomes readily apparent that Adam had abandoned his responsibility of properly teaching Eve not only the command of God, but the practical application of its usage.

Don't judge or condemn Adam, though. Many of us have equally abdicated the responsibility of leading our loved ones in this area as well. Even worse, there are multitudes of us who have not even taken the responsibility to learn the Word, ways and culture of God ourselves.

I had this very discussion with a friend of mine on the eve of this writing. His family is in utter chaos. When I pointed out that he is abdicating his God-given responsibility to spiritually lead his family, he readily admitted it. He knew it and he understood this. He had just not taken the responsibility to have dominion over his home.

Instead of love, he was attempting to bully his family into the results he desired. That is not dominion. It is belligerence and the result will always be chaos. *"The kingdom of heaven suffers violence..."* If this is you, simply repent, apologize to your family, learn the Word of God, and go forward. The objective is not to beat yourself up for what you have not done in the past. The goal is to move forward and to encourage yourself and your family to go forth with God, to become a part of God culture. You can never go wrong when you go forward with God. You can then turn the tables on Satan and take the kingdom back by force. Remember, you have been given absolute authority over the situation.

Let's Go to the Videotape

You may be wondering how I have surmised that Adam had abandoned his responsibility. To answer this, let's rewind the videotape and go back to the original command about the tree of the knowledge of good and evil. Then, let's examine Eve's response to the serpent.

"Then the Lord God took the man and put him in the Garden of Eden to tend and to keep it." Take note of what man's function on the earth was intended to be: to tend and to keep. That would have been nice...huh! *"And the Lord God commanded the man, saying, 'Of every tree of the Garden you may freely eat; but of the tree of the knowledge of good and evil **you shall not eat**, for in the day you eat of it you shall surely die."* (Genesis 2: 15-17) Remember what is highlighted within this Scripture, *you shall not eat.* This is exactly what should have been taught to Eve. "Eve, don't eat it. If you do, you die, period!"

Now, let's examine Eve's response and her misunderstanding of God's command, or Word. I will also show you what I truly believe to be the downfall of all humanity. There is something not necessarily expressed, but certainly implied, that continually, even to this day, leads us to our very own downfalls. Satan not only knows it but he is an expert at using his influence to capitalize on it.

"And the serpent said to the woman, 'Has God indeed said, you shall not eat of every tree of the Garden?'" The number one tool Satan uses to attack mankind is to question and cause you to doubt the authority of God and His Word. This is exactly what he is doing here. In essence, he is testing her understanding and belief. Do you remember in one of the previous discussions in the earlier chapters how Satan steals from those who lack understanding? You are about to experience the greatest heist in all of human history and, perhaps, in the history of the entire universe.

> *"And the woman said to the serpent, 'We may eat of the trees of the garden;* (so far so good) *but of the fruit of the tree which is in the midst of the garden, **God has said,*** (pay attention) *'You shall not eat it, **nor shall you touch it**, lest you die.'"*
> **—Genesis 3: 1-3**

Refer back to what I asked you to note above. When did God say that Adam and Eve could not touch the fruit? That is absolutely correct; He did not. God did not say one word about touching the fruit. He simply said, "Do not eat it." This may seem like small potatoes or nitpicking, but it was enough for Satan to decide that Eve was the one to attack and not Adam. Had she voiced an understanding, I believe he would have most likely moved on to either another target, meaning Adam, or what is even more likely, another tactic.

However, that would not be necessary. He immediately perceived that he could deceive Eve. The same holds true for *you* when you fail to gain an understanding of the Word and ways of God. Understanding the Almighty is the entire premise of this book. It is the reason I have written it. You cannot win without understanding, and you cannot understand without a relationship with the Creator.

The more beaten-down people I meet, the more I realize the reason for their inability to properly function in their God-given gifts. It is nearly always the result of their misunderstanding of God's character and nature due to their lack of understanding God's Word. They have no cultural reference point.

It is like trying to communicate in a language you do not even speak. Without a translator, it is impossible to connect under such circumstances, and, therefore, the separation from God remains, and thus the problems. Sometimes, and what is a more serious issue, however, is their outright rebellion and refusal to be subject not just to His, but to anyone's, authority. If that is you, I would encourage you to simply let go of your pride. Pride is nearly always a tremendous hindrance to receiving the help you need.

The God given gifts that I am referring to here are not just gifts within the church. They are gifts within your job or business, community, household, family, friends, ministry and more, as well as the church. Every talent you have is a blessing given to you by God. Therefore, every blessing or talent you possess is not just a physical gift, but a spiritual gift as well— if you are functioning properly within God culture.

However, there is an even greater problem that we must learn to recognize. Adam and Eve never did. They could not because of their inability to perceive evil. They had no barometer for it before eating the forbidden fruit, and that is important to realize when you find yourself judging Adam.

Evil was always present in the Garden. We know that because Satan as well as the tree of the knowledge of good *and evil* was present in the Garden, but Adam and Eve had no perception or acknowledgment of evil due to their lack of sin. In other words, before the evil of sin entered into their being, they had no ability to perceive or receive it. It was foreign to them. They would not have recognized it if it hit them in the face… and man, did it ever.

Hanging Around the Wrong Tree

Have you ever wondered why we are so drawn to evil? It was no different for Adam and Eve. Although the Word doesn't say that, it doesn't have to. Their actions proved it. Additionally, I don't have to know you or any other man to have an understanding of your nature because it is the same as mine. The fact that they were drawn to evil is implied by the very fact that they were hanging around the wrong tree, just like we do, and this is the problem. This is where Adam abdicated his responsibility, and this is also where *we* relinquish ours.

They had permission and access to every tree in the Garden of Eden, yet the tree they chose to continually hang around was the only one they were not supposed to and could not have. We seem to have this idea that the Garden of Eden was about the size of our backyards and that they could not escape the presence of the tree of the knowledge of good and evil. Nothing could be further from the truth.

This was an entire land, complete with four rivers, mountains, forests, and more. Do you know of any rivers that encompass the length of your backyard? Most are hundreds of miles long. There was only one forbidden tree located in the center of the *entire* garden, and, of all places, that is where they decided to camp out! They did not just stumble upon it by happenstance either; they without a doubt had to actively seek it out. So you tell me: were they drawn to evil? You're darn right they were! It was the only tree, and probably the only *thing,* in the entire garden that was forbidden to them. Sound familiar? Can you see yourself in this picture?

Jesus taught us to pray, "*…and lead us not into temptation, but deliver us from the evil one.*" Ultimately, the fall of man was not the result of willful disobedience. It was the result of hanging around the wrong tree and from allowing themselves to *remain* in the presence of temptation rather than moving on to something else. If you give the devil a ride in the back seat, it won't be long before he's driving. Don't be fooled; if you hang around the wrong tree long enough, it won't be long before you're eating from it.

Not only should Adam not have been hanging around that tree, he should have been diligently instructing and, yes, forbidding his wife of the same. Unfortunately, however, it would not have worked. They were too infatuated with what they could not have, and all too often so are we.

In case you are wondering, this was the only place that Satan had access to them. It is also the only place he gains access to you. We do not see Satan attacking them anywhere else in the Garden. He couldn't. He had no control of them without the fruit of sin. In fact, what we see elsewhere is, *"…the sound of the Lord God walking in the Garden in the cool of the day…"* (Genesis 3: 8)

Curiosity Killed the Cat

Implanted deep within the nature of every human being is something called "curiosity." It causes us to desire knowledge. It was intended for us to desire the knowledge of God but, as a result of free will, it also causes us to be drawn to the things we are forbidden to have, those things we do not know but long to learn about.

I have heard a multitude of sermons and read a plethora of articles pertaining to the subject of man's fall. In most, you will find the reason for the rebellion as being Adam's passivity, or his refusal to take authority, or whatever passive/aggressive symptom that manifested itself that day. They are all partially correct but these are only symptoms. They are outward manifestations of a deeply rooted inner problem.

The truth is, and what you have most likely never heard before, is that the root cause for the fall of man was curiosity. Curiosity has two sides, a light side and a dark side. When a human being maintains a close relationship to his Creator, the gift of curiosity is an immensely powerful and positive tool. When allowed to run amuck, it is dark and destructive. You have heard the saying, "Curiosity killed the cat." In this instance, curiosity killed the human race! I will show you why I surmise this shortly. Don't fret, for as we will see, God had and still has a "forever" plan.

A Gray Area

In returning to our story, the serpent is not quite finished yet. At this point, Adam and Eve are not so innocently hanging around with the devil. Don't judge; this is quite common. They think they can get away with it. Even worse, they even think God doesn't know. Just like you and me, they have fallen prey to Satan and they are about to be caught in a trap. They will also have absolutely no comprehension of the consequences until it is too late.

"*Then the serpent said to the woman, 'You will not surely die. For God knows on the day you eat of it your eyes will be opened, and you will be like God, knowing good and evil.'*" (Genesis 3:4-5) These two sentences give us tremendous insight into the method Satan uses to entrap us. There are three truths in these sentences and two lies. Pay attention to this because the reason Satan has the ability to ensnare us is due to his uncanny ability to be cunning, while at the same time being astonishingly subtle. He's no idiot. He may be unrepentantly evil but he is no idiot.

Let us begin with the lies Satan told. Number one, he promised Eve that if she trusted him she would not die, and number two, he promised Eve that she would be like God. Let's compare these to the truth. Number one, he promised Eve she would not die. Number two, he promised Eve she would be like God... and no, that is not a typographical error. He *is* that tricky. Number three, her eyes would be open to know good and evil.

If the above sounds a bit confusing or perhaps even eerily similar, it is intended to. Satan's influence lurks within the gray areas of life, oftentimes making it difficult to distinguish the truth from a lie.

What did Satan do? He peaked her curiosity. Once that job was done, he used a tool even more powerful against the human race than a nuclear bomb. As a matter of fact, not only is this Satan's nuke, it is most likely the reason we have even created nuclear weapons. Once you push the button, you have lost. The launch sequence begins and you have a lifetime battle on your hands. His nuclear warhead, which he has launched at every person in human history, is pride. He appealed to her pride. The instant he won that appeal, he moved on to her ego. With that one conquered, the battle had been won. She now belonged to him. She had become his slave.

He convinced Eve that there was something God had that she did not. In essence, he said to her, "Eve, God is keeping something from you. He has something very good and He does not want you to have it. Eve, can't you see that you're blind? He is keeping you in the dark. Follow me and I'll give you light. I'll open your eyes. Then you will be just like we are. It will be me, you and God."

In fact, at that very moment Satan *became* Eve's god. Her pride and his lie overrode the truth of God and she perceived the serpent to be her provider. I cannot stress enough the importance of recognizing when this is occurring in your life. I encourage you to be aware and keep your ego out of it. Nothing will remove you from God culture faster than pride and ego.

This trap is so common that in America we have a saying for it. We call it, "Keeping up with the Jones'." It means that our pride and our ego cause us to feel the need to have what everyone else has, whether we can afford it or not and whether it is good for us or not. If we don't get it, we feel inferior.

Evil was an item that Adam and Eve could not afford to have. The cost was too high. The devil's cost is always too high. It seems logical at first and it may even seem good. Certainly Satan's offer to Eve seemed good at the time. It had to have because she accepted it. Eve did not know evil. She had no frame of reference, and she did not understand the consequences. Neither do you if the Word of God is not firmly implanted in your heart. Outside of God culture, the world is a gray area.

Subtleties

With that said, let's return to the lies Satan told Eve. He began by promising her that if she ate the fruit she would not die. Let's examine this. Was it a lie? This may surprise you but the answer is both yes and no. How about the second attempt, "You will be like God." Was that a lie? Whenever I ask that question, people automatically shout, "Yes, that was a lie!" Was it? I told you Satan was cunning. I told you he was subtle. I also told you he was no idiot but that's not really true. He is a total idiot. Anyone who would intentionally rebel against God is a complete knucklehead, especially with the position he held in heaven and the knowledge of God he possessed... but he *is* subtle. Let me show you just how cunning and subtle he actually is.

Let's fast-forward to the point just after Eve ate the fruit and passed it to her husband, Adam, so he could also eat it. Now their eyes open up. They see evil for the first time and it changes the very nature of their being. In fact, being the perversion of the Holy Spirit that Satan is, it actually fills them. Evil *is* the spirit of Satan.

We now find them hiding from God's presence, placing the blame on others and, for the first time, feeling guilt and shame, which, unless you have committed some horrendous crime, is never from God. God then rebukes and curses the serpent. He rebukes Eve and He rebukes Adam. *"Then the Lord God said, 'Behold, **the man has become like one of Us,** to know good and evil...'"* (Genesis 3:22)

Look at that again and I will ask you one more time: Did Satan lie to Eve? Again, the answer is both yes and no. What Satan actually does is tell half-lies. Did Adam and Eve become like God? The answer is still both yes and no. Yes, because their eyes were opened. They now know evil. For the first time in their lives, they have the ability not only to recognize it, but to participate in it as well. In fact, unbeknownst to them at the time, they just did. They committed an evil act against the Lord without even knowing what they were doing. Think about that in reference to your own life. It is not an excuse for sin.

On the other hand, no, they did not become like God because they can never be as powerful and wise as God; they can never be a God; and, in fact, they wound up losing all of the authority given to them *by* God. In reality, by believing and obeying Satan's lie, they actually became *less* like God. This will always be the case with Satan. He is the deceiver of the brethren and nothing good ever has, ever will, or can come from him.

His goal is to steal, kill, and destroy, in that order. (John 10:10) He wants to steal you from the kingdom of God, kill you before you have the opportunity to repent, and destroy your everlasting spirit and soul for eternity. Do not fall for it. Allow God to be God and He will free you and save you. His arms are wide open, ready and willing to receive you.

The Bear Trap

While we are on the subject, allow me to illustrate something about sin. In the Word of God, sin is oftentimes regarded as a "snare". What exactly is a snare? It is not just a trap. Psalm 91 states that "... *surely He will deliver you from the snare of the fowler.*" You see, in biblical times they used to use snares to hunt small birds and animals. Even today, many hunters still use some type of trap.

Let's imagine for a moment that you are this happy little animal frolicking through the forest when all of a sudden, "**whack!**" The trap snaps shut and you're stuck. Ensnared! You never saw it coming. It was subtly camouflaged beneath the surface and now you are stuck. Every struggling move you make only causes the trap to dig deeper into your flesh, ripping and tearing to the bone. With every pull and tug, a seething pain rises up to your torso. You begin to lose blood. You are feeling faint, and you do not quite realize what is happening.

From afar you begin to hear the rustling of bushes. Twigs and branches begin crackling and snapping. Something is moving toward you. You begin to panic. Your attacker draws near. Your heart races as adrenaline fills your system. You are thrashing wildly in a futile attempt to break free, but the trap… It won't open. Think fast. Do something. Hurry … release the trap! Too late….

The Woodsman

When caught in this type of trap, an animal has several very limited options. Number one, and let's assume that the pursuer, or hunter if you will, has not shown up. Your first option is to wait. Maybe somehow you will get free. The only problem here is that you have no food, no water, and an injury that is eventually going to become infected and fester. You will succumb to one of these three ills if ensnared long enough.

Number two, wait until your pursuer appears. This obviously leads to death as well. He ensnared you for a reason. Option three: chew your leg off. Even if you succeed, you will most likely bleed to death. If you are unfortunate enough to survive being ensanguined, your injuries will cause you to either be killed and/or consumed by another animal, or you will starve to death due to your inability to hunt. These are the only options that the snare of sin leads to. They all result in death.

There is one more option available. You can be fortunate enough to have a compassionate and merciful "Woodsman" who cares enough to free you from the trap, bind up your injuries, and nurse you back to health. You may be a bit wounded, but you will most certainly recover.

That compassion and mercy only lies in Christ. He is that Woodsman! Only *He* can release you from the trap of sin. Good deeds cannot do it. Sacrifice cannot do it. Only He can deliver you from the snare of the fowler. If you are reading this, you can take this moment to repent. Allow the Savior, Jesus Christ, to free you. He will do so willingly and unconditionally. Just take a moment right now and ask Him. Don't be afraid; *"…cast your sin upon Him, His yoke is easy and His burden is light."* (Matthew 11:29) Or if you would prefer, you can just ignore Him and chew your leg off. It's your choice.

If you have repented, then find a Bible and begin reading it. I would strongly encourage you to find a faith-filled Church and get connected. You can also find a discipleship group to stay connected and share your life with. That is God's plan and a major part of God culture.

Thus far, Satan has done nothing but separate you from God and the fellowship of other believers. This is exactly what he did to Adam and Eve. He separated them from God. Like any good general, his goal is to divide and conquer. Certainly you can see his work in the world today. Mankind is deeply divided on nearly every front. Do not participate in it.

Do you realize that we have not even gotten to the second lie yet? We do need to go there because there is more to learn. So let's dive back in.

Deceived or Disobedient

"Then the serpent said to the woman, 'You will not surely die...'" (Genesis 3:4) Was this a lie? Once again, the answer is both yes and no.

Have you ever noticed that people can tell you about their experiences but it never truly resonates unless you actually encounter it on your own? It is the stupidity of youth. God explained death to Adam. Without a doubt, God explained death to Adam. I am even convinced that Adam and/or God explained death to Eve but neither Adam nor Eve had ever seen anything die. They had no working knowledge or experience with the concept.

There is no finality in eternity. Therefore, when Satan told Eve she would not die, the Word says that unlike Adam who was simply disobedient, Eve was genuinely deceived. She actually believed it. Remember though, Adam is close by, watching this whole scene play out. In fact, he is within an arm's length. Eve simply reached back and gave Adam the fruit.

There is one thing we misunderstand about Adam. He was truly created in God's image. Since the Word says *God is love*, Adam was also made in the image of Love. Therefore, Adam had to have had a deep love and an immensely compassionate relationship with Eve. Why then would he allow this serpent, that he knew was attempting to kill his wife, to continue in this manner? I believe there is only one possible answer. It had to be curiosity.

Adam knew that the fruit of this tree would cause death, but he could not have known what death truly was. He could not have conceptualized its permanence. So he must be standing there thinking, "Okay, let's see what happens when she eats it. What will happen after she dies?"

Heck, people have had this thought since the beginning of time. The issue of finality was inconceivable to Adam. Nothing had ever died. Consequently, Adam allows the conversation to continue and does not interfere when Eve decides that the fruit must be good for them since it will make one wise. Even though he is most likely thinking, "This serpent is full of... baloney."

Have you ever followed anyone or made a stupid decision based on something someone said whom you knew was full of baloney? C'mon, at one time or another, we have all done it. It is the same situation here. Remember, Adam was not deceived but simply disobedient. He is curious to see what's going to happen. Think about it. If someone were attempting to kill your wife, would you simply stand by and watch? Sorry folks, but if that happens in my house, "it's on!" So he watches as Eve eats the fruit.

Guess what happened? She didn't die... well... not immediately. Unbeknownst to either one of them, she *began* to die. They just could not see it. They couldn't feel it. They couldn't hear, taste or smell it, and since she did not just fall dead to the ground... Ker plunk! As Adam must have expected, he also makes the decision to obey the serpent and he eats it too. Although neither one of them fell to the ground dead, they begin to experience the symptoms of spiritual death. They became acquainted with shame, guilt, and, most notably, separation from the presence of God.

So did Satan lie? You're darn right he lied! He told the worse kind of lie there is. Not the kind designed to preserve oneself, but the kind designed to destroy another human being.

Don't Play With Fire

Do you still think you can play with the devil and win? Jesus didn't even try it. He exclaimed, *"Away with you, Satan."* (Matthew 4:10) He did not play around and try to reason with the devil. Do you think you can dabble with evil and not get hurt? I must tell you the truth. Adam and Eve were a better man and woman than we are. They were created without sin and still became ensnared by it, even though they physically walked hand in hand with God each and every day.

You are just the opposite. You have been born into sin. You entered the world with a nature that was wontedly attracted to evil and is separate from your Creator. Therefore, you must diligently labor to ward it off. Yet you still believe you can hang around the tree? It will not work. Don't play with fire.

Banished

Now I've said all of this to bring you to the following point. *"Then the Lord God said, 'Behold, the man has become like one of Us, to know good and evil.*

And now, lest he put out his hand and take also of the tree of life, and eat, and live forever'— therefore the Lord God sent him out of the garden of Eden to till the ground from which he was taken. So He drove out the man; and He placed cherubim at the east of the Garden of Eden, and a flaming sword which turned every way, **to guard the way to the tree of life.** *"* (Genesis 3: 22-24)

It is always at this point that our misunderstanding of God reveals itself. It appears on the surface that God is angry with Adam and Eve and, as a means of punishment, He banishes them from the Garden. However, nowhere in the Scripture does it say that God became angry with them. We just automatically assume that He is because we have been programmed from childhood to believe that God is that big angry puppet master that I alluded to in paragraph one of this chapter. Let's examine what God actually said. The key is in the following sentence. *"And now, lest he put out his hand and take also of the tree of life, and eat,* **and live forever....** *"*

Once again, we see God abruptly cutting off His sentence. It is as if He could not allow Himself to finish. I stated earlier that whatever God says comes to pass. What was it that God was about to say? I have to believe that based upon the circumstances of the situation that just occurred, He was getting ready to say something along the lines of, *"And now, lest he put out his hand and take also of the tree of life, and eat, and live forever* **and his sin along with him...**"

That would have been a disaster! It would have solidified sin in mankind for all of eternity and would have immediately resulted in permanent spiritual death. Since God is love, He discontinued His speech.

So what did God do? He ended His sentence and banished the man from the Garden of Eden. Was He angry and frustrated with him? Was it a means of punishment? This is what most of us believe. The answer however, is one hundred percent, absolutely **not**! It was not punishment; it was **mercy**! How was it mercy? Read on and discover the true nature of God culture.

The Tree of Life

Let's step back for one second. What most of us do not realize is that in order for Adam and Eve to live forever, it was imperative for them to eat from the tree of life. As a matter of fact, when the Lord recreates heaven and earth and the New Jerusalem descends out of heaven from God to take root in the New Earth, He will reinstitute the eating from the tree of life.

If that sounds incredulous to you, just step back for a moment and think. In your present condition, do you have to eat to live? Of course you do. Otherwise you will suffer malnutrition and starve to death. In eternity, you will not be a disembodied spirit. You will have a glorified body that will still require nutrition but you will not eat the corrupted death-producing trans-fats brought into the world as a result of sin. Remember, where there is no death, there will be no animal matter to eat.

In fact, man was not given the authority to eat meat until after the flood of Noah. Furthermore, it is hypothesized that the first animals ever killed were those sacrificed by God to clothe Adam and Eve after they sinned. In eternity, there will be no death so you will eat the same glorified fruit and vegetable matter that Adam and Eve ate in the Garden of Eden. You see this does not cause death to the plant. The plant can drop a seed or shoot a root and continuously propagate. When an animal or anything that contains "the breath of life" is extinguished, however, death is the result. This will not occur in eternity.

Take note of this glimpse into eternity contained within the Book of Revelation. *"And He showed me a pure river of water of life, clear as crystal, proceeding from the throne of God and from the Lamb. In the middle of its street, and on either side of the river, **was the tree of life,** which bore twelve fruits, each tree yielding its fruit every month. The leaves of the tree were for the healing of the nations. And there shall be no more curse, but the throne of God, and of the Lamb shall be in it, and His servants shall serve Him. They shall see His face..."* (Revelation 22: 1-4)

Everlasting Life

At the very moment sin entered mankind, it became a *requirement* for man to die. Had God allowed Adam to continue eating from the tree of life, and had God allowed mankind continual access to the tree of life, man would have lived forever. Why is that a problem? If a fallen humanity, full of sin and iniquity, were permitted to live forever, then sin would also live forever.

Perhaps you are thinking, "So why would that be a problem? I am not so bad." Maybe you are not, but can you imagine living in a world where men like Adolph Hitler or Joseph Stalin could not die? How might that culture evolve? How about Jeffrey Dahmer or John Wayne Gacy? What about Emperor Nero, who would casually impale Christians, light them ablaze and use them as torches to light the Roman streets? What about the worst possible offenders of humanity you can imagine?

Death is mercy. God was not punishing Adam and Eve. He was saving them. He was acting in mercy while at the same time, however many thousands of years ago that was, He was also being merciful to you. The gift of death, given to mankind by God, is what allows your sin to be blotted out. Death is not the end. It is a new beginning. Mercy is the root of God culture. It always leads to forgiveness.

To sum it all up, if man were not able to die, a certain Savior named Jesus Christ would have been unable to die as well. This would have rendered God powerless to remove your sin. You see God's eternal plan was even at work in the perfection of the Garden of Eden. When God used the gift of death and sacrificed Jesus on the cross, He laid your sin upon Him. When Jesus died, your sin, which became a part of Him, also died.

When God raised Him up, Jesus eternally left your sin in the pit of hell, never to be seen again. Now you can *truly* be like God, sinless and eternal. Take a moment today to thank God for His everlasting mercy. As always, the mercy of "Now vs. Forever" lands right in the middle of God culture.

— CHAPTER 8 —

More Mercy!

"For the Lord is good; His mercy is from everlasting, and His truth endures to all generations." (Psalm 100:5) Without God, I am pretty sure that mercy is a quality that would no longer exist in mankind, not in the world and not even in your own home. I oftentimes cannot even find it in myself. I am just being honest.

Without God, mankind has become basically selfish and generally unforgiving. Without the fear of God, which incorporates a fear of judgment, why not do whatever you would like whenever you like? This is how the world is beginning to live. It has become the New World culture and not just in America; it is affecting the entire planet. Many believe as Robert A. Heinlein does that, "Theology is never any help; it is searching in a dark cellar at midnight for a black cat that isn't there. Theologians can persuade themselves of anything."

I must say that this breakdown in human thought is utterly unacceptable. I believe that true mercy can only be found within the pages of the Bible. Most do not realize that mercy is a reciprocal act. In order to receive mercy, one must practice it. In order to practice mercy, you must first receive mercy.

By the end of this chapter and discussion, God is going to reveal His goodness and mercy to you and in the process you are going to perhaps learn something brand new. The Lord Almighty is about to switch places with you. He will remove the responsibility of giving mercy from His shoulders and place it squarely upon *yours*. Do not be afraid of this. That is what covenant partners do and He has given His Spirit to help you. This is a necessary aspect of your relationship with Him. It is an integral part of not just entering but remaining within the bulwarks of God culture. In the end, it is designed to make you free. So if you're ready to receive mercy, and I know you are, read on.

In previous chapters we learned that we oftentimes misunderstand God's actions due to our miscomprehension of His character. Most of us have had the misconception that the Lord was punishing Adam and Eve when He expelled them from the Garden of Eden.

In reality, we learned that it was actually mercy and not punishment, due to the fact that God needed to restrain them from partaking of the tree of life. In this chapter, let's take a closer look at the fact that not only do we all require God's mercy, but that it is also the desire of His heart; no, let me rephrase that, it is His very nature to *bestow* it upon you. First, let's make sure that we all understand a few things about our Messiah. Let's examine the following claims Jesus made in Scripture.

Just Tell Me

"Now it was the Feast of Dedication in Jerusalem, and it was winter. And Jesus walked into the temple, in Solomon's porch. Then the Jews surrounded Him and said to Him, 'How long do You keep us in doubt? If you are the Christ, tell us plainly.' Jesus answered them, 'I told you and you do not believe... I and My Father are one.'"

—John 10:22-25 & 30

It is quite obvious who Jesus was claiming to be in this Scripture. As a matter of fact, in order to leave no doubt as to Jesus' meaning, the next sentence states the Jews took up stones to stone Him. (John 10:31)

The Jews of Jesus' day had absolutely no doubt about what Jesus was claiming. However, all their outburst did was confirm Jesus' original premise that they did not believe Him. They were attempting to stone Him for blasphemy. To make oneself equal to God was blasphemous in Jewish culture. That is, unless you actually are the God you assert yourself to be, which is exactly what Jesus was laying claim to. No other Jewish "prophet" had ever attempted this before that time, and this statement of boldness and confidence, as well as His ability to change the direction of humanity, confirms the validity of His declaration.

"Then Philip said to Him, 'Lord, show us the Father, and it is sufficient for us.' Jesus said to him, 'Have I been with you so long and yet you have not known Me, Philip? He who has seen Me has seen the Father; so how can you say, 'Show us the Father?'" (John 14:8-9) Once again we see Jesus boldly proclaiming that He is God.

Here's more. *"Do not be afraid; I am the First and the Last* (the Alpha and Omega). *I am He who lives, and was dead, and behold, I am alive forevermore. Amen. And I have the keys of hell and death."* (Revelation 2:17-18)

Here we see the resurrected Christ after being returned to His rightful place of glory, boldly proclaiming His Deity as being the Alpha and Omega, the First and the Last, the Beginning and the End, which is a testament to His everlasting and eternal nature.

This infinite characteristic can only belong to the one and only living God, Jehovah, who is Christ the Lord. Only Jehovah possesses the keys to hell and death. Only Jehovah is the beginning and the end of time. He and Christ are one. No other prophet has ever made this claim... not Buddha, not Joseph Smith, and not even Mohammed; no one. Why is that? Jesus Christ alone is worthy to claim it. He alone is the way, the truth and the life. He alone is God.

*"He has delivered us from the power of darkness and conveyed us into the kingdom of the Son of His love, in whom we have redemption through His blood, the forgiveness of sins. **He is the image of the invisible God,** the firstborn over all creation."*

—Colossians 1:13-15

*"God, who at various times and in various ways spoke in time past to the fathers by the prophets, has **in these last days** spoken to us by His Son, whom He has appointed heir of all things, through whom also He made the worlds; who **being the brightness of His Glory and the express image of His person,** and upholding all things by the Word of His power, when He had Himself purged our sins, sat down at the right hand of the Majesty on high..."*

—Hebrews 1:1-3

The purpose of the preceding Scriptures is to lay the foundation for illustrating the following characteristic of God to you. I am speaking of the wonder of His mercy. Since Christ is the express image of God, He is also the express image of mercy.

Therefore, in order to illustrate this characteristic, I will show you an incredible act of forgiveness and mercy on the part of Jesus Christ of Nazareth. The aforementioned material was to illustrate beyond any shadow of doubt who Christ has claimed to be and, in fact, who He actually is. When you see Christ, you see the Father. Therefore, when you see the actions and personality of Jesus Christ, you are seeing the actions and personality of the Father, who is Jehovah (or YHWH), expressed to and in the form and image of humanity.

He is the expressed image of God's mercy. Do you find this illogical? We have already discussed why Christ in the flesh was actually the most logical resolution to sin. How else could we comprehend such complex wisdom and power unless He brought it to our level? Soak up the following excerpt from the Word of God. You are about to witness the pinnacle of God culture. In order to do so, I would like to introduce you to the one and only Jesus Christ of Nazareth, the Messiah.

Everybody Must Get Stoned

> "Now early in the morning He came again into the temple, and all the people came to Him, and He sat down and taught them. Then the scribes and the Pharisees brought to Him a woman caught in adultery. And when they had set her in the midst, they said to Him, 'Teacher, this woman was caught in adultery, in the very act. Now Moses, in the law, commanded us that such should be stoned. But what do you say?' This they said, testing Him, that they might have something of which to accuse Him. But Jesus stooped down and wrote on the ground with His finger, as though He did not hear.
>
> "So when they continued asking Him, He raised Himself up and said to them, 'He who is without sin among you, let him cast the first stone.' And again, He stooped down and wrote on the ground. Then those who heard it, being convicted by their conscience, went out one by one, beginning with the oldest even to the last. And Jesus was left alone, and the woman standing in the midst. When Jesus had raised Himself up and saw no one but the woman, He said to her, 'Woman, where are those accusers of yours? Has no one condemned you?'
>
> "She said, 'No one, Lord.'
>
> "And Jesus said to her, 'Neither do I condemn you; go and sin no more.'
>
> "Then Jesus spoke to them again saying, 'I am the light of the world. He who follows Me shall not walk in darkness, but have the light of life.'"
>
> **—John 8:2-12**

Let me begin with the accusation by the scribes and Pharisees. Please understand that this was a Jewish woman. If otherwise, she would not have been bound to the law. As a result, she knew where her fate would lie if caught.

In addition, the Pharisees came to Jesus claiming that the woman was caught in the very act of adultery. I have no doubt that this claim was true because neither Jesus nor the woman disputed it. You will also notice that

Jesus was neither appalled nor surprised by this woman's sin. Whether you realize it or not, He is neither appalled nor surprised by yours either. Just as this woman was caught in the very act and commission of such an exploit, so are you. You cannot hide it. God knows what you are doing while you are in the very act. He even knows before it has been committed or even thought of, and yet He does not "stone" you.

I find Jesus' reaction to the scribes' accusations quite interesting. He simply ignored them. He stooped down on the ground and acted as if He did not hear a word they were saying while seemingly scribbling in the sand. What was Jesus doing? What was He writing? Wouldn't you love to see a videotape of this scene? Perhaps one day when we are in heaven, we will be permitted to watch the videotapes of such scenes. I would love to see what Jesus was writing; however, I think I have a clue.

Glass Houses

Let's use our God-given gift of imagination for just a few minutes. I want you to thrust yourself back in time for a moment and pretend that you are among the crowd of students Jesus was teaching. Picture yourself dressed in your tunic. What color is it? I'll bet most of us say white. We have all watched way too many movies. (You probably think it's clean too. Do you think Jesus had Woolite®?)

It's hot. It's dusty. The arid desert sun burns your skin. You are with Jesus in the midst of the temple when all of a sudden you hear a commotion. You hear a woman ranting and an angry mob of fallen humanity flailing and dragging the desperately resistant mistress toward the place of Jesus' instruction.

Suddenly, all those gathered turn toward the bedlam. You begin to move in the direction of the commotion with Christ as your guide. When the crowd reaches you, several heavily bearded men in priestly attire thrust the woman to the earth in the midst of the gathering.

She despondently curls herself into the fetal position, futilely attempting to hide her shame and nakedness while tears and sobs emit her mortification. Her tattered clothing, or lack thereof, tells the story of her guilt. The men begin pointing and bellowing their murderous accusations in the direction of the Messiah. The confluence eagerly awaits His condemnation, but amazingly He does not even respond. He simply remains silent, stoops down and begins scribbling in the dust.

The Pharisees begin pressing Him. The more they press, the more He writes. However, the mood of the crowd begins to wane. They begin to see the words scrawled faintly into the dusty granules. As they gaze upon their own transgressions depicted before them, they see the words… liar, deceiver, hypocrite, thief, amongst a plethora of others.

Jesus rises up and proclaims, "Let he who is without sin among you cast the first stone!" He again lowers Himself and continues the list… cheater, fornicator, adulterer, and more. One by one you begin to hear the thumping of stones emanating upon the ground. With heads dropping in shame and self-disgusted guilt, the crowd slowly disperses and the love of Christ begins to piece together the life of a broken woman. She enters God culture.

His loving gaze pierces her. "Woman, where are your accusers?" With tears running down her soiled face, she proclaims, "They are no more, my Lord." "Neither do I accuse you either, my daughter… go and sin no more."

Public Defender

If you have never met Him, you have just been introduced to Jesus Christ of Nazareth. There is no other like Him. Perhaps for the first time, you have come face to face with mercy, and with love. These two attributes go hand in hand. You will not find one without the other. God is love and God is mercy. He is also much more.

When looking at this story as a whole, a couple of things jump out right away. First of all, she *is* guilty, caught red-handed. Secondly, Jesus defends her. This is quite interesting. We know this woman was an Israelite. Otherwise, she would not have been bound to the law and the entire scene would have never taken place. I bring this up as a point of encouragement to you. I point to the simple fact that her Hebrew heritage entitled her to a defense with the Almighty serving as her attorney, and what a job He does.

Do you realize that when you accept Jesus as Lord and you become a part of God culture, you are adopted into the same family and become entitled to the same defense by the same Defender?

*"But when the fullness of time had come, God sent forth His Son, born of a woman, born under the law, to redeem those who were under the law, **that we might receive the adoption as sons.**"* (Galatians 4:4-5) You become a spiritual Israelite. *"To You, O my Strength, I will sing praises; **For God is my defense, My God of mercy.**"* (Psalm 59:17)

What we actually witness in this story is a picture of the Lord standing in the gap and defending us against the accusations of Satan. The woman represents you and me, the precious family of Yahweh and an adulterous nation of sinners chasing after the pleasures of life. The Pharisees represent the prideful accuser of the brethren, Satan. It is Jesus alone who stands between him and us.

> *"Then I heard a loud voice saying in heaven, 'Now salvation, and strength, and the kingdom of our God, and **the power of His Christ have come,** for **the accuser** of the brethren, who accused them before our God day and night, has been cast down. And they overcame Him by the blood of the Lamb and by the word of their testimony....'"*
> **—Revelation 12:10-11**

Do you know the Lord died to adopt you? He died to defend you. He suffered to make you whole in God culture. Most of us may never realize that we are as guilty as the woman caught in adultery. In God's eyes, we have been "running around" behind His back and fraternizing with the gods of greed, money, Hollywood, and the lusts of the flesh.

We may also never realize that all the guilt and shame can be wiped away in an instant. We don't need to fall into the final hands of the Omega. The Lord longs for you to reach out to the merciful arms of the Alpha and begin anew with Him. The incredible beauty of His mercy is that you do not have to wait one more minute to do so. There is no need to clean up, sober up, or whatever you may think would please Him. Just simply believe and He will take care of the rest.

Close Encounters of the Sin Kind

Let's reexamine the preceding text. There is quite a bit more to learn about the Lord from this passage. In John 8:2, we are first introduced to Jesus in the temple functioning as a teacher. This is what Christ does. *"But you, do not be called 'Rabbi'; for One is your Teacher, the Christ."* (Matthew 23:8) *"However, when He, the Spirit of truth, has come, He will guide you into all truth...."* (John 16:13) He teaches and leads us into the truth.

In the preceding story, we find the scribes and Pharisees encountering a truth we must all experience when coming face to face with Christ. That experience is what I would call a "close encounter" with our own sin. Every human that has a genuine introductory experience with Jesus will be convicted of sin. This is an act of mercy and kindness on the part of our Creator. In order to experience true repentance, there must be the *recognition and acceptance* of one's faults or shortcomings.

What I find truly amazing is to what extraordinary lengths the Lord will go in order to gain our attention. In the preceding case, it took the mortifying experience of being caught "red-handed" in adultery, followed by public humiliation, for the woman to accept her own iniquity. Does the Lord need to resort to such extreme measures in order to make an initial connection with you? Maybe not, but unfortunately, for many of us, the answer is yes.

Congruently, it took the adultery of a sinful woman to confront a plethora of equally abhorrent lifestyles within the mob of Pharisees. Both resulted in conviction of sin and both were designed to bring repentance. Both were the loving actions of a merciful Creator. Which would you prefer, a little pain now, or an eternity in hell? God still works all things together for good for those that love Him. Sometimes even for those who don't. Who are we to argue with what He deems to be correct?

We always focus upon the love and compassion Jesus had for the woman caught in adultery and that is certainly the truth. However, the gospel is that Jesus had just as much love and compassion for the crowd of murderous stone throwers. He just needed to use a different method to gain their attention.

The wonders of God are endless. Who else could orchestrate such a scene? Who else could put together such a cast of characters and design a two-thousand year old mob scene in which we continually experience our own transgressions to this very day? William Blake said, "The glory of Christianity is to conquer by forgiveness."

Take careful note of how this story ends. Jesus makes the statement, "Neither do I condemn you." It is imperative to understand that Jesus did not come here to condemn us. He came here to save us. You also must remember your end of the covenant. Jesus truly did not condemn this woman. However, with forgiveness comes responsibility. Along with mercy comes culpability. *"Go and sin no more. He who follows Me shall not walk in darkness, but have the light of life."* The light of life is mercy; the lack of forgiveness is darkness. If you want to live for God, if you want to be a part of God culture, then you must practice mercy.

Forgive Us Our Trespasses

Let's learn more about mercy. Our God *is* Mercy. The word "mercy" actually means to be compassionate and forgiving. For one to be merciful, they must have a *disposition* of being compassionate toward an offender, enemy, or another person whom you have power over, such as a judge who is lenient or even forgiving in his sentencing of one being found guilty in the commission of a crime. As we have seen earlier in Adam, and in the case of the woman caught in adultery, this describes God's nature to perfection.

For man, mercy is a conditional characteristic. For God, it is without partiality. I did not say that mercy is without condition. God's *love* is unconditional, meaning that He loves you no matter who you are or what you have done, but His mercy has two conditions. You must accept Jesus Christ and you must practice mercy toward others.

The Lord went through excruciating pain and humiliation to redeem you from the curse of sin and death. You cannot receive it any old way you choose. *"There is a way that seems right to a man, but its end is the way of death."* (Proverbs 14:12) God made a way to salvation. He made a way for you to obtain mercy. You must do it *His* way. *His* only conditions are that you accept the gift of life that He provided for all of humanity in the person and sacrifice of the Lord Jesus, and that you share that mercy with others.

You see, a man may feel merciful one day and unmerciful the next. A man may feel like loving you one day and hating you the next. A man may be faithful one moment and unfaithful the next. A man may even be truthful in one situation and lie in another. God never waivers in this manner. *"For the Lord is good. His mercy is everlasting and His truth endures to all generations."* (Psalm 100:5)

However, in order to receive mercy from the Lord, it is imperative that you obey the following examples from the Word of God. Take note of the following account taken directly from the mouth of Jesus.

You're the Man

> *"There was a certain rich man who had a steward, and an accusation was brought to him that this man was wasting his goods. So he called him and said to him, 'What is this I hear about you? Give an account of your stewardship, for you can no longer be steward.'*
>
> *"Then the steward said within himself, 'What shall I do? For my master is taking the stewardship away from me. I cannot dig; I am ashamed to beg. I have resolved what to do, that when I am put out of my stewardship, they may receive me into their houses.'"*
> **—Luke 16:1-4**

I find it amusing that most of the folks I talk with about this Scripture have the same reaction. I also believe the disciples Jesus was speaking with probably had the same reaction as well. At this point in the story most of us are thinking, "Man, this dude is in troubl-l-l-l-l-e! He messed *up.*"

Let me tell you that Jesus is not speaking of some fictional steward. A "steward," as used here, is someone who manages the affairs or property of another. Jesus is speaking directly to you as a "steward" in this passage, for if you are a believer in the Lord Jesus Christ then *you are* the steward. You are a steward of the gifts that God has given you. This includes your talent, intelligence, emotional wellbeing, spiritual life, family, friends, job, ministry, and, once you have accepted Christ, the Word of God as well. Thank God the Holy Spirit is within us to help us manage such numerous responsibilities.

Are you properly managing the affairs and responsibilities the Lord has given you in this life? Do you even know what they are? If not, you are wasting the Lord's goods.

After reading this, you may have the same reaction David had to the Uriah incident when the Prophet Nathan opened David's eyes. Let's take a look at *that* situation for guidance.

> *"It happened in the spring of the year, at the time when kings go out to battle, that David sent Joab and his servants with him, and all Israel; and they destroyed the people of Ammon and besieged Rabbah. But* **David remained in Jerusalem.**
>
> *"Then it happened one evening that David arose from his bed and walked on the roof of the king's house. And from the roof he saw a woman bathing, and the woman was very beautiful to behold. So David sent and inquired about the woman. And someone said, 'Is this not Bathsheeba, the daughter of Eliam, the wife of Uriah the Hittite?' Then David sent messengers and took her... and lay with her..."*
>
> **—2 Samuel 11:1-4**

There are several issues within this piece of Scripture, and the adultery and/or fornication of David is obvious, notwithstanding. Number one, David was in a place that he should not have been. Home! To use an illustration that we discussed earlier, he was "hanging around the wrong tree." Do you remember that discussion? He was supposed to have gone out to battle with his soldiers. However, David chose to remain behind in Jerusalem.

Then one evening, due to his obvious boredom, and perhaps worry over a situation he could no longer control, and being unable to sleep, he decides to go up on the roof of the palace to take a walk. Lo and behold, he takes the bait of Satan. He sees a gorgeous woman bathing and begins to fantasize about her.

May I make a suggestion to you married folks? It is one thing to look. It is quite another to dwell and begin fantasizing, which is obviously what David began to do because he had his servants go get her. You must look away. Do not hang around the tree. Don't even make eye contact, if you want to stay out of trouble. I understand that you are still a man and recognize a beautiful woman when you see one. That is normal but do not let it go any further.

If you already have, go to God for forgiveness. The covenant between yourself, your God, and your wife is much more important than the passing pleasure of beauty and lust. Jesus taught us to pray, *"…and lead us not into temptation, but deliver us from evil."* (Matthew 6:13) This begins by controlling the eyes and the mind.

David, however, is the king, a man of power and authority. When he gives the command, they go and get her. All you men of power better *beware!* This is a highly prized trap of the devil. Since David is the king, and the king can do whatever he wants, or so men of power believe, David sleeps with her. He knew she was married, and he knew her husband who happened to be one of his closest generals and is listed amongst the names of David's legendary mighty men. But it's "good to be the king!" It's good to be a man of power. Isn't it?

"…and the woman conceived; so she sent and told David and said, 'I am with child.'"(2 Samuel 11:5) Uh oh! Then David did the right thing. He confessed to Uriah and took care of Bathsheeba and the child for the rest of their lives. Right? **Wrong!**

"Then David sent to Joab saying, 'Send me Uriah the Hittite.' When Uriah had come to him, David asked how Joab was doing, and how the people were doing, and how the war prospered. And David said to Uriah, 'Go down to your house and wash your feet.' So Uriah departed… but Uriah slept at the door of the king's house… So David said to Uriah, 'Did you not come from a journey? Why did you not go down to your house?'"

This is a feeble attempt by David to cover his sin. He figured if he could get Uriah home, he would sleep with his wife and David would be off the hook. He could then claim the baby was Uriah's. Even if it came out looking just like David, there was no DNA testing back then, and who would dare to second-guess the "integrity" of the king?

> *"And Uriah said to David, 'The ark and Israel and Judah are dwelling in tents, and my lord Joab and the servants of my lord are encamped in the open fields. Shall I then go to my house to eat and drink, and lie with my wife? As you live, and as your soul lives, I will not do this thing.'"*
> **—2 Samuel 11:6-11**

This should have been David's reaction while his men were at war. Instead of showing love for God and loyalty to his soldiers as Uriah did, David took Uriah's wife, and as you will see later, his life. David grossly underestimated the loyalty and integrity of Uriah. Uriah was a great man and we can learn a tremendous amount from his loyalty. He was firmly entrenched in God culture.

However, David still has a problem. Rather than face the consequences, rather than show mercy to a man under his power, David, the king of Israel, sends his good friend and loyal protector Uriah the Hittite to the front lines of the battle to die, knowing that his return was impossible. Problem solved. Over and done with; but wait, there is one more problem. David seems to have forgotten about God.

> *"Then the Lord sent Nathan to David. And he came to him and said to him, 'There were two men in one city, one rich and one poor. The rich man has exceedingly many flocks and herds. But the poor man had nothing, except one little ewe lamb which he had bought and nourished; and it grew up together with him and his children. It ate of his own food and drank from his own cup and lay in his bosom; it was like a daughter to him. And a traveler came to the rich man, who refused to take from his own flock and from his own herd to prepare one for the wayfaring man who had come to him; but he took the poor man's lamb and prepared it for the man who had come to him.'*

*"So David's anger was greatly aroused against the man, and he said to Nathan, 'As the Lord lives, the man who has done this shall surely die! And he shall restore fourfold for the lamb, because he did this thing and because **he had no pity.**'*
"Then Nathan said to David, 'YOU ARE THE MAN!'"...
—2 Samuel 12:1-7

Smack... smack, smack, smack! Talk about a rebuke. Talk about being convicted. Talk about having been blind to the truth. This is the same reaction I have when I read the parable of the unjust steward that we examined above. God has given us so many blessings, gifts and responsibilities, and oftentimes we simply waste them away.

Have you ever had the same reaction as David, only to find you have been guilty of that which you have accused another of, that "You are the man," as Nathan so aptly phrased it? I have. How should we react? It's simple, run to God. Receive mercy and then show mercy. Get yourself right back into God culture. Any other reaction is simply laboring in vain.

As We Forgive Those...

There are two types of sin, and, no, I am not talking about mortal verses whatever. Those types of sin do not exist. In God's eyes, there is no large or small sin. There is only sin. There are two categories in which you can *commit* a sin. There are sins of "commission," such as David, Uriah and Bathsheeba, and there are sins of "omission," such as wasting the Lord's goods, refusing to acknowledge Him, praise Him, pray, worship, believe, and others.

Both are sins and both will destroy your life if left unchecked. David committed both types in this instance. His sins of commission were against Bathsheeba and Uriah and also God. His sin of omission was his selfish refusal to recognize his own sin and his unmitigated lack of mercy due to self-preservation.

"...the kingdom of heaven is like a certain king who wanted to settle accounts with his servants. And when he had begun to settle accounts,

one was brought to him who owed ten thousand talents (this is equal to many millions of dollars). *But as he was not able to pay, his master commanded that he be sold, with his wife and children and all that he had, and that payment be made. The servant therefore fell before him, saying, "Master, have patience with me, and I will pay you all. Then the master of the servant was moved with compassion, released him, and forgave him the debt."* (This is a picture of you and me and our relationship with God through Christ.)

"But that servant went out and found one of his fellow servants who owed him a hundred denarii (which is equivalent to pennies) *and he laid hands on him and took him by the throat, saying, 'Pay me what you owe!' So the fellow servant fell down at his feet and begged him, saying, 'Have patience with me and I will pay you all.' And he would not, but went and threw him into prison till he should pay the debt... Then his master said to him, 'You wicked servant! I forgave you all that debt because you begged me. Should you not also have compassion on your fellow servant, just as I had pity on you?' And his master was angry, and delivered him to the torturers until he should pay all that was due to him.*

"So my heavenly Father also will do to you if each of you, from his heart, does not forgive his brother his trespasses."
—Matthew 18:21-35

Jesus taught us to pray, *"Forgive us our trespasses as we forgive those who trespass against us."* (Matthew 6:12) What does this mean? It means that the same measure of forgiveness you use in having compassion on others, God will have on you. You must learn to forgive completely. If you are merciful to others, God will be merciful to you. That's God culture and here is why.

All of us have sinned against God. He is the "king" in the above Scripture. We are the servant. We must forgive the debts of others because God forgave an immense debt that we owe Him. We can never repay our debt to Him. He forgave us so completely that we have an eternal place in heaven when we make Jesus our Lord.

Therefore, we *must* show the same compassion to others that God has shown to us. God died a torturous death on the cross because of His love, compassion, and desire to be one with us. His death was a substitution for ours. He bled and died and through it all He never stopped showing mercy, even toward those who were pounding the nails through His hands.

> *"And when they had come to the place called Calvary, there they crucified Him, and the criminals, one on the right hand and the other on the left. Then Jesus said, 'Father, forgive them, for they know not what they do.'"*
> **—Luke 23:33-34**

A Promise to Marry

Look how close the Lord desires to be with you. *"I will betroth you to Me forever; yes I will betroth you to Me in righteousness and justice, in loving kindness and mercy. I will betroth you to Me in faithfulness, and you shall know the Lord."* (Hosea 2:19-20)

The word "betroth" means to arrange for a marriage. Its archaic meaning, in which time Hosea was written, actually means a promise to marry. The Lord will never divorce His beloved people. Marriage is the essential component of every culture and it is the defining element of God culture.

God has promised and arranged to wed you but you must accept His proposal. That is the arrangement the Lord has made. Say yes to Him and you will receive mercy, to dwell with Him in the glory of the New Jerusalem forever. He will forgive your sins and you will find sanctuary in the kingdom of God. He is mercy. Welcome to the everlasting kingdom of God culture.

Conclusion

Although you have come to the end of this book, your journey is just beginning. I have no doubt that you have come to see God in a new way, but, believe it or not, you are just catching a glimpse of His greatness. The relationship and the revelation He has for you is unique to who you are, and His will is for *your* very own life.

Therefore, as He continues to reveal Himself to you, I would encourage you to be diligent in your pursuit of His presence. As you enter into God culture with Him, He will fulfill your every dream and desire. Do not be fooled, though. It will not be easy. He will not just wave a magic wand and make everything go away. There will be challenges to overcome, but keep in mind that nothing of any real value is easy to obtain. Changing the world through God culture is no exception to this truth.

To assist you in getting to know Him even further, the *Understanding the Almighty* series has been prepared to help you continue your walk with Him and achieve your eternal destiny. In *Yahweh Revealed*, you will get a closer look at who He is and how you can enter into a more intimate relationship with your Creator.

Once there, it is time to begin looking at some of the great mysteries of life, death and God. Therefore, I have created *Secrets of the Father* to bring you to a greater understanding of the ways of Almighty God. My prayer is that you will come to a deeper understanding of the Lord and His ways and that you will fulfill your ultimate destiny in God culture by becoming a disciple of Jesus Christ of Nazareth.

May the Lord bless you in all that you do!

About the Author

John A. Naphor is a husband, father of three children, and currently a partner in a thriving wealth management business. John's experiences include serving as a missionary to the Indonesian community in the United States and Canada. He has also been involved with an apostolic ministry which has planted churches from Toronto, Canada, to Atlanta, Georgia, and as far west as Los Angeles, California. John has ministered as close to home as his local church and as far away as Jakarta, Indonesia, a nation containing the largest Muslim population in the world.

CPSIA information can be obtained at www.ICGtesting.com
Printed in the USA
BVOW04*2022160314

347714BV00004BA/24/P